WAIT 'TIL NEXT YEAR

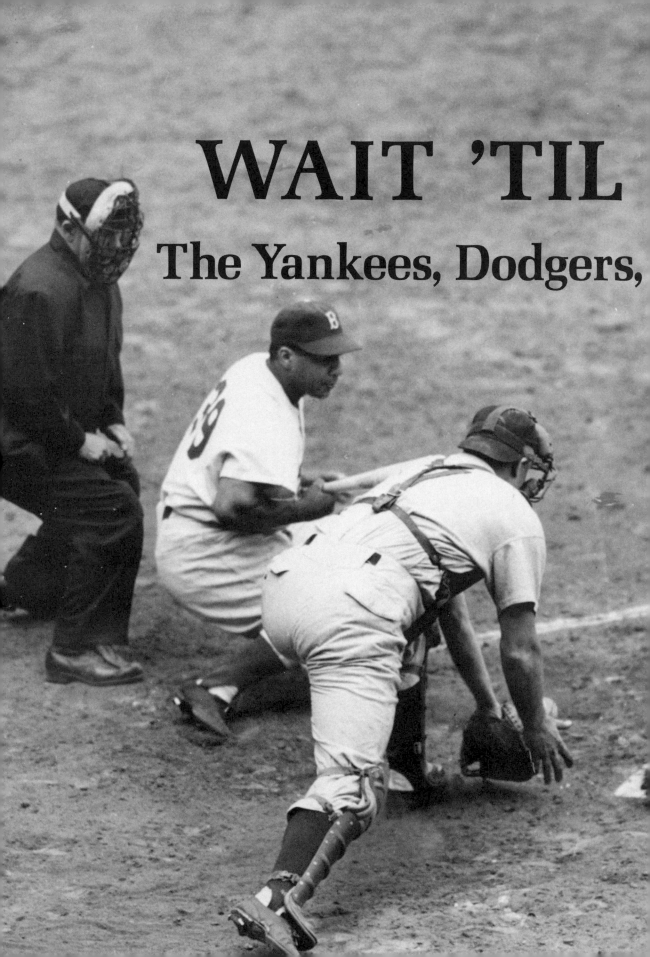

WAIT 'TIL
The Yankees, Dodgers,

CHRISTOPHER JENNISON

NEXT YEAR

and Giants 1947–1957

W · W · NORTON & COMPANY · INC ·
NEW YORK

Copyright © 1974 by W. W. Norton & Company, Inc.

FIRST EDITION

Library of Congress Cataloging in Publication Data
Jennison, Christopher.
Wait 'til next year.
Includes bibliographical references.
1. Baseball—Pictorial works.   2. New York (City).
Baseball club (American League)   3. Brooklyn. Baseball
club (National League)   4. New York (City). Baseball
club (National League, Giants)   I. Title.
GV867.3.J46   796.357'09747'1   74–8030
ISBN 0–393–08696–8

Published simultaneously in Canada
by George J. McLeod Limited, Toronto

This book was designed by Robert Freese.
Typefaces used are Times Roman and Melior Semi Bold.
Manufacturing was done by The Haddon Craftsmen, Inc.

PRINTED IN THE UNITED STATES OF AMERICA

1 2 3 4 5 6 7 8 9 0

For Annice, Clark, and Edmund
with gratitude, admiration, and love

Contents

Acknowledgments

Most of the research for this book was conducted at the Goldfarb Library at Brandeis University, the Cary Memorial Library in Lexington, Massachusetts, and the Boston and New York Public Libraries. At all times I was the beneficiary of efficient and accommodating services. I am also grateful to Cliff Kachline for his many courtesies during the time I spent at the National Baseball Library in Cooperstown, New York. Helpful too was Marty Appel, the assistant director of public relations for the New York Yankees, who promptly and cheerfully responded to my requests and queries.

Picture research was aided greatly by considerate people at Wide World, Brown Brothers, UPI, Time-Life, and especially the New York *Daily News,* where Gene Ferrara permitted unrestricted access to his indispensable photo library.

Many thanks are due my friend Ralph Protsik, who was sensible and unflinching in his criticisms. My editor at Norton, Evan Thomas, expressed enthusiasm throughout the project, and was a constant source of precise and constructive guidance. Although they didn't realize it, Allie Reynolds and Don Newcombe lent moral support at a pivotal time during the book's progress. Finally, I cannot adequately express my gratitude to Keith Jennison, who provided at all the right times the invaluable observations of a shrewd editor and the loving encouragement of a father.

Introduction

At Yankee Stadium on October 10, 1957, the Yankees lost the seventh game of the World Series to Lew Burdette and the Milwaukee Braves. Burdette completed a masterly performance—three complete game victories, the last two shutouts—in leading his team to the world championship, a prize that had been the exclusive property of New York baseball teams for the previous eight years.

It was a gloomy finale to a dismal year in New York. Two months earlier the National Exhibition Company, the corporation operating the New York Giants, voted to transfer the franchise to San Francisco in time for the 1958 season. On October 8 the Dodgers announced their plans to move to Los Angeles, and two days later the invincible Yankees were toppled.

Franchise shifts had been accomplished by the Braves in 1953 and by the Athletics and Browns shortly thereafter. But unlike fans in Boston, Philadelphia, and St. Louis, who had seemingly shrugged off the losses of their teams, many thousands of Giant and Dodger worshipers felt betrayed and knew that baseball would never be quite the same again. Gone were the teams that for more than seventy years had represented the National League in New York with distinction, controversy, and beguiling eccentricity. Only memories remained, memories made more poignant by the sense of loss. John McGraw, Christy Mathewson, Bill Terry, Carl Hubbell, Willie Keeler, Dazzy Vance, Babe Herman, Pete Reiser, and scores of more recently celebrated heroes became distant dreams. The city had been severed from a fundamental link to its proud traditions. The other cities had lost baseball teams; New York had lost part of its soul.

This book will describe in pictures and words the New York baseball scene from the beginning of the 1947 season to the end of the 1957 World Series. During this eleven-year period professional baseball in the city reached a peak of national dominance. Only once in this time did a New York team fail to reach the World Series, and on seven occasions two city teams were represented.

The interborough rivalries boiled and attendance figures soared. There were frenzied races; not preludes to divisional play-offs, but real down-to-the-last-game, nail-biting, joyously climactic pennant races. And the tension of subway Series gripped the city.

It would be too space-consuming to try to list all the memorable players in this prologue, but inevitably a certain few evoke their own special magic: Joe DiMaggio, Jackie Robinson, Phil Rizzuto, Peewee Reese, Yogi, Campy, Allie

Reynolds, Sal Maglie, Preacher Roe, Mickey Mantle, and Willie Mays. This was the time of Mickey and Willie in their resilient youth, throwing and running and hitting with awesome grace and power.

Here too will be some of New York's non-playing baseball fraternity, who made their own unique contributions: Red Barber, Russ Hodges, Mel Allen, Happy Felton, Gladys Goodding, the Dodgers' Sym-Phony, and the unmatched New York fans.

A special photo-essay is devoted to the stadiums, particularly the Polo Grounds and Ebbets Field, both of which were razed with dismaying ease and overnight supplanted by anonymous brick high-rises. How very special these ball parks were! In this present time of antiseptically precise arenas virtually undistinguishable from one another, they persist in the memory as peculiar and delightful, suitable and personal. By today's standards Ebbets Field was impossibly small. But the players could be seen without binoculars, and home runs did not land anticlimactically in a grassy moat between fences, but instead fulfilled the wildest of youthful fantasies, disappearing from sight over the grandstand, into Bedford Avenue, through someone's window, or onto a passing truck. *That* was a home run!

Uptown, at the foot of Coogan's Bluff, stood the Polo Grounds, shaped like a huge bathtub, perfect for football or polo, but providing a baseball field with a Sahara in center field and foul poles that could be reached by bat boys. Across the Harlem River Yankee Stadium still stands, and will always be the "big ball park" for generations of New Yorkers.

Obviously, not all of the great stars of that time were members of New York teams. In the chapters that follow we will meet again Stan Musial, Ted Williams, Ralph Kiner, Bob Lemon, Robin Roberts, George Kell, Warren Spahn, Billy Pierce, and Richie Ashburn. And those with encyclopedic memories may recognize fleeting figures of somewhat lesser stature.

On the cover of the 1952 Giants yearbook, Willard Mullin drew a cartoon of Leo Durocher reading to an oversized and dreamy-eyed ballplayer. The name of the book was *The Little Miracle of Coogan's Bluff,* and the player is wistfully saying, "Read it to me all over again, Leo." There are quite a few of us who feel that way about New York when it boasted three exciting baseball teams and the game itself had not become a relentlessly dollar-motivated industry.

Christopher Jennison

Preface

by Dick Young

Each of us remembers something else. You remember where you were when Bobby Thomson hit his historic homer to put the Giants into the 1951 World Series? I remember that I was in the Polo Grounds press box, tearing up a page and a half of breathless prose that told of how the Dodgers had beaten the Giants.

Do you remember where you were in 1954, when the Giants swept the Indians in the World Series, blitzing a team that had piled up 111 victories during the season—when teams played only 154 during the season. I remember sitting next to Hank Greenberg during Game 4. Hank was vice-president of the Indians then. He and his friend, Bill Veeck, were running the ball club, and were in slight shock. If anybody was supposed to win four straight, it was the Cleveland Indians, with starters like Bob Lemon, Early Wynn, Mike Garcia, and Bob Feller. The Giants had Johnny Antonelli, Sal Maglie, Ruben Gomez, and—Don Liddle?

But there it was, the Giants ahead 3 games to 0, and Hank Greenberg no longer thinking about winning the World Series. All he wanted was Game 4, so that there would be Game 5, the Sunday game. There would be 80,000 people in the Wigwam for the Sunday game, and the Indians needed that. The players' kitty gets most of the money from the first four games of any World Series. It must go five for the ball clubs to start making a profit.

"We're going to air-condition all our offices with the money from Game 5," I remember Hank Greenberg saying. "That's why we have to win today. We just have to."

The Giants put the early slug on Bob Lemon, taking a 7–0 lead, but Cleveland fought back, scored three on Don Liddle, then another, and suddenly Game 5 became a viable vision in Hank Greenberg's thoughts again. He looked down to the Giant bullpen.

"He wouldn't!" gasped Greenberg. "Leo wouldn't do that to us, would he?"

Warming up was Johnny Antonelli, ace southpaw who, just two days earlier, had beaten the Indians, 3–1, blanking them through the final eight innings. Greenberg couldn't conceive of Leo Durocher relieving with Antonelli, of trying to crush them four straight.

But Leo could, and did. Antonelli came in to shut the door the last two innings, and there went the air-conditioning.

These are the warming memories that come back to me as I drift through the eleven years of baseball history written by Chris Jennison, those eleven surreal seasons, when New York dominated the world of baseball. New York had numbers going for it, because it had three teams in the bigs. For each of those eleven years, except once, New York had a team in the World Series, often both. Invariably, it was the Yankees. Usually, it was the Yankees playing the Dodgers. And a couple of times it was the Giants.

But New York had more than numbers, more than just three teams. It had three outstanding teams, spiced with outstanding characters, men of tremendous prowess, from the tips of their nimble fingers to the depths of their loud larynxes. They had Leo Durocher and Charlie Dressen and Casey Stengel. They had Willie Mays and Eddie Stanky, Joe DiMaggio and Jackie Robinson. They had the big achievements, and the little human touches. As I breeze through Chris Jennison's fast-moving history, *Wait 'til Next Year,* those wonderful little touches come back to me. So often, they are the little things that led to the big things:

That day in Havana, March 1947. Other than the wartime training camps of the North, ersatz experiences at best, this was my first of what spring training was like. Imagine that. A young, goggle-eyed newsman, in exotic Cuba with the eccentric Brooklyn Dodgers. That day they were playing the Yankees, who had flown over from Florida.

Manager of the Dodgers was Leo Durocher. General manager of the Yankees was Larry MacPhail. Larry and Leo hated each other from the last picture.

"Look at that!" exclaimed Leo the Lion, pacing the Dodger dugout like a lion. "If I did that, I'd be thrown out of baseball!"

Leo was looking into the box seats, near the Yankee dugout. There sat Larry MacPhail, and there, separated from him by an aisle, sat a well-known gambler. Durocher was wondering aloud about a double standard. He had been warned by Commissioner Chandler about associating with certain gambling types. Was it all right, demanded Durocher, for Larry MacPhail to associate with men who were precluded from the life style of Leo Durocher?

Leo made such a noise, reproduced in the newspapers, that a hearing resulted—and, sure enough, Leo Durocher was kicked out of baseball, for one year.

I can remember, later that day, the day Durocher made his accusation against MacPhail, leaving the press box to go down to MacPhail's seat and ask him to reply to Leo's charges.

"Is this man with you?" MacPhail was asked.

"He's in another box," said MacPhail.

"But is he your guest?"

Larry MacPhail's parched and heavy lower lip quivered with repressed anger. "You're not the district attorney!" he shouted, calmly for him. "I don't have to sit here and be cross-examined by any ess-oh-bee like you! Now get the hell out of my box!"

"I thought I was doing you a favor, trying to get your side," said the rookie reporter, trying to act brave, but truly intimidated. And with that, I got the hell out of his box.

1948. Another year, another exotic training grounds. This time, the Dodgers

set up camp in the Dominican Republic. Leo Durocher had been reinstated by Chandler. During spring training, in order to open up second base for Jackie Robinson, the Dodgers trade Eddie Stanky to the Boston Braves. (That's right, kids; the *Boston* Braves.)

Muggsy Stanky is shocked. He had worshiped at the shrine of Leo Durocher, the man he called "The Lion," with all the nobility and kingsmanship the word suggests.

"The Lion has stabbed me in the back!" quoth Ed Stanky.

Newsmen carried the message back to Leo, who replied, "I need Stanky like I need a third eye!" Baseball, it turns strong friends into bitter enemies overnight.

The year was not too far along when Durocher suffered a deeper shock. Branch Rickey traded him to the Giants. For nothing. That can dent a man's ego.

Women roll better with the punches. Mrs. Durocher at the time was Laraine Day, the film star from the original Dr. Kildare days, and a willing baseball fan. When newsmen found her at home, and broke the news to her, she walked into the living room, where the radio was blaring the Dodgers' game. "I guess I have the wrong game on," she said coolly, flicking the dial to the Giants' broadcast.

I suppose no year in New York baseball annals can match 1951. The Yankees won in the American League. The Giants and Dodgers tied in the National—the three-game play-off that was to be decided by Bobby Thomson's sudden-death home run.

Earlier in that season, there was another Giant-Dodger game at the Polo Grounds. Carl Furillo drove a liner to right center labeled extra bases. The Giants' center fielder streaked into the alley, one-handed the drive. Billy Cox tagged at third and broke for home. The center fielder, whirling in a 360-degree turn upon making the catch, uncorked an on-the-fly peg to home, where Wes Westrum, with the plate nicely blocked, slapped the tag on the startled base runner. Willie Mays, through the rest of his days, was to call that the finest defensive play of his life.

After the game, the suddenly unjaded newsmen swarmed around Charlie Dressen in the Dodger clubhouse. And what did Brooklyn's manager think of that catch-and-throw by the Giants' rookie?

"I gotta see him do it again," said Chuck, always a bit reluctant to praise players on the opposing team. There were no instant replays in those days. Dressen meant Mays had to make the play again to convince him he was that good.

Two years later, 1953, the Dodgers, midway through the race, pulled away from the Giants, and Dressen, in his sublime confidence, uttered another immortal line. "The Giants is dead!" he said in singular grammar. This not only provoked Giant fans to screaming anger, it touched off a debate among the world's literati on the proper use of the plural verb. At least one English professor rushed to Dressen's support, insisting that "Giants," being a collective noun, may well take a singular verb.

At any rate, Dressen was right in substance. The Giants was dead, and the

Dodgers again went into a World Series, to take another beating from the Yankees. It wasn't till 1955, with a kid named Johnny Podres mixing smoke with a precocious change-up, and Sandy Amoros one-handing a high fly down the left line by Yogi Berra, that Brooklyn finally beat the Yankees; that Brooklyn won its first World Series. It was to be its last.

The Brooklyn Dodgers expired after the 1957 season, a losing year, but before that they were to get one more shot at the Yankees. That is the year, of course, they ran into Don Larsen's perfect game. Larsen was known to celebrate, even when there was nothing particular to celebrate. He would wind up, occasionally, at a little bar on Fifty-seventh Street owned by Bill Taylor, an outfielder with the Giants.

Bill Taylor had a bartender who played golf left-handed, which happened to be an affliction of mine. One day, I loaned him my left-handed golf clubs. He told me, the next night, he thought the clubs were great. I told him I thought they were lousy. He said he would bet me $100 against my golf clubs that the Yankees beat the Dodgers in the World Series. I said, "You're on."

Next to Larsen's perfect game, that is what I remember best about the last Subway Series played in New York. I lost my golf clubs as the Yankees beat Brooklyn, 4 games to 3. It was the best bet I ever lost. I gave up playing golf.

Dick Young

WAIT 'TIL NEXT YEAR

Jack Roosevelt Robinson on April 11, 1947, the day the Dodgers purchased his contract from the Montreal Royals. Later that year he was named Rookie of the Year by the *Sporting News*, in 1949 he was the National League's Most Valuable Player, and in 1962 he was elected to the Hall of Fame. *N.Y. Daily News Photo*

CHAPTER ONE

1947

Jackie Robinson and the Birth of the New York Dynasty

New York and Brooklyn's period of baseball preeminence began at the start of the 1947 spring-training session with the arrival of more than a dozen talented rookies and first-year men and the return of established regulars from military service. All three teams profited substantially by the replacement of wartime standins. Joe DiMaggio and Tommy Henrich of the Yankees succeeded Tuck Stainback and Bud Metheney, Peewee Reese and Pete Reiser replaced Eddie Basinski and Goodie Rosen in the Dodger lineup, and Johnny Mize and Walker Cooper were back at the Polo Grounds, making it necessary for Phil Weintraub and Clyde Kluttz to seek employment elsewhere.

The new men included Larry Berra, Allie Reynolds, Vic Raschi, Bobby Brown, Frank Shea, Ralph Houk, Larry Jansen, Wes Westrum, Clint Hartung, Johnny Jorgenson, Edwin "Duke" Snider, Gil Hodges, and Jackie Robinson.

Jack Roosevelt Robinson was twenty-eight years old at the time the Dodgers brought him up from their Montreal farm team. He had already spent two years preparing for his major-league debut by developing, under Dodger owner Branch Rickey's tutelage, the capacity to tolerate hostilities certain to accompany his promotion. Rickey's counsel served him well during the first weeks of spring training, when Jackie's teammates contemplated a walkout and fans in southern cities hooted their objections to his presence.

At that time more than 60 percent of the active major-leaguers either lived or had been born in the South. It was Peewee Reese, a resident of Louisville, Kentucky, who went out of his way to make Robinson feel welcome. Reese's gesture failed to pacify the red-necks among the spectators, but it did help discourage further team dissension.

Just as conditions in the Brooklyn camp were stabilizing, Dodger manager

Mel Ott, a Polo Grounds legend, and in 1947 the manager of the Giants, is shown here welcoming Clint Hartung, the "Hondo Hurricane," as he reported to New York for the first time. Hartung had fabulous advance notices but never quite lived up to them. *UPI Photo*

Left: The Dodger captain, Harold "Peewee" Reese, and Harold "Pete" Reiser, who hit .343 in 1941 but had his career shortened by injuries, a few of which were the result of collisions with outfield fences. *N.Y. Daily News Photo*

Right: Polo Grounds power. This trio —left to right: Walker Cooper, Johnny Mize, and Willard Marshall— combined for 122 home runs and 367 RBIs in 1947. *UPI Photo*

Leo Durocher was suspended for the season by baseball commissioner A. B. "Happy" Chandler. Leo had earlier accused Yankee president Larry MacPhail of keeping company with known gamblers, and when Durocher charged that Chandler maintained a double standard toward MacPhail, the Commissioner suspended Leo for the rest of the year, citing "conduct detrimental to baseball." Leo was replaced for one game by coach Clyde Sukeforth, who wanted no part of the job and was relieved when Rickey named Burt Shotton to be the full-time Dodger skipper.

Before joining the Dodgers, Jackie Robinson had played shortstop and second base for the Kansas City Monarchs in the Negro League and later with Montreal. But Reese and Eddie Stanky were set in those positions, so on opening day Jackie was the Dodger first baseman. He went hitless against the Boston Braves in the opener at Ebbets Field, but three days later belted his first homer in his second time at bat at the Polo Grounds. The Dodgers traveled to Philadelphia, where Jackie tried to ignore vile bench jockeying by the Phillies, and particularly by their manager, Ben Chapman. In St. Louis the defending World Champion Cardinals threatened to boycott the opening game of the series with the Dodgers, then finally showed up and spent three days insulting the Brooklyn rookie. A measure of revenge was gained at the end of April, when the Dodgers reached first place while the Cards were losing eight straight games and sinking into the cellar.

The Giants, who had finished last in 1946, delighted their fans by staying close to the top of the standings during the first half of the season. Johnny Mize, Walker Cooper, and Willard Marshall terrorized opposing pitchers, while Larry Jansen, who had completed a 30–6 season for San Francisco in the Pacific Coast League in 1946, and lefty Dave Koslo pitched well. At the All Star break the Polo Grounders were only a game and a half out of first.

The hitters stayed hot all season, but Jansen and Koslo could not indefinitely shoulder the entire pitching burden. The team wilted in August, lost eight games in a row, and finished the season in fourth place, twenty victories improved over 1946. Johnny Mize's fifty-one homers led the team to a single-season record of 221 home runs, but the team also led the league in errors and its pitchers posted the league's second highest earned-run average. Hope for the future, however, was sustained by Larry Jansen's 21–5 record and the fine play of twenty-four-year-old Bobby Thomson.

The Yankees, trying to better their third-place finish of the previous season, limped through the first few weeks of 1947 without the injured Joe DiMaggio. When Joe returned, the Bombers proceeded to make a shambles of the rest of the league. They won nineteen consecutive games in midseason, built a twelve-game lead over their closest pursuers, and coasted to the pennant, their fifteenth since 1921. While the hitters could not compare with the Giant sluggers for sheer muscle, DiMaggio, Tommy Henrich, and George McQuinn contributed numerous game-winning hits, and the pitching staff, paced by Allie Reynolds, Frank Shea, Spud Chandler, and reliever Joe Page, was the best in the American League.

During late July the Dodgers nearly duplicated the Yankee runaway with a thirteen-game winning streak that provided a ten-game lead over the Cardinals. But the Redbirds halved the lead by mid-September, setting up a critical three-game series in St. Louis. All three games were decided by one run, but the Dodgers won two and maintained a safe lead the rest of the way.

Shortly before the third Cardinal game, the *Sporting News* named Jackie Robinson the National League's Rookie of the Year. Jackie's credentials were impressive: he hit safely in twenty-one straight games during July, batted .461 during the crucial September series in St. Louis, led the league in stolen bases, and finished the season hitting .297. He developed into a sure-handed first baseman, established an intimidating baserunning style, and opened the way for two more black players: Larry Doby of the Indians and Dan Bankhead of the Dodgers.

Jackie was given a "Day" at Ebbets Field two days after the Dodgers clinched the pennant. Among the many gifts was a new car, the keys to which were presented by entertainer Bill "Bojangles" Robinson, who quipped, "I'm sixty-nine years old, but never thought I'd live to see the day that I'd stand face to face with Ty Cobb in technicolor."

The World Series had not been played in New York for three years; an equivalent lapse would not occur for more than two decades. The 1947 championship was the first to be televised, and two sponsors bid a total of $65,000 to advertise their products. Liebmann Breweries pledged $100,000, but Commissioner Chandler rejected their bid, maintaining that it would be bad for baseball's image to have the World Series sponsored by the purveyor of an alcoholic beverage.

The first two games at Yankee Stadium attracted more than 140,000 spectators, most of whom were delighted with a pair of Yankee victories. Frank Shea and Joe Page combined to win the opener, 5–3, when twenty-one-game winner Ralph Branca weakened after retiring the first twelve Yankee batters. Shoddy play in the field by the Dodgers in the second game allowed Allie Reynolds to coast to a 10–3 triumph, his first World Series win. After the opener Yankee

The New York Yankees' lineup for the opening game of the 1947 World Series. Left to right: Bucky Harris, manager; George "Snuffy" Stirnweiss, second base; Tommy Henrich, right field; Yogi Berra, catcher; Joe DiMaggio, center field; George McQuinn, first base; Billy Johnson, third base; Johnny Lindell, left field; Phil Rizzuto, shortstop; and Frank "Spec" Shea, pitcher. *N.Y. Daily News Photo*

A rookie battery for the Yankee Series opener. On the left is Frank Shea, also known as the "Naugatuck Nugget." His catcher is Yogi Berra, beginning a nineteen-year career with the Bronx Bombers. *N.Y. Daily News Photo*

Cookie Lavagetto smacking Bill Bevens' pitch against the right-field screen at Ebbets Field. It simultaneously broke up Bevens' no-hitter and won the fourth game of the World Series for the Dodgers. *N.Y. Daily News Photo*

manager Bucky Harris was asked if he had made any special preparations for the Dodgers. He shrugged and said, "We went over the lineup. But it was the usual kind of meeting, the same as if we were going over the Browns."

At Ebbets Field the Dodgers fought back and won the third game, 9–8, chasing veteran Bobo Newsom from the mound with a six-run second inning. The Yankees rallied on a home run by DiMaggio and the first pinch homer in Series history, hit in the seventh inning by Yogi Berra, but Hugh Casey relieved at that point and held the Yanks in check the rest of the way.

With his fingers crossed, Bucky Harris sent Bill Bevens, a 7–13 operative during the regular season, to the mound for the fourth game. Bevens was provided a 2–0 lead in the fourth inning, gave up a run to the Dodgers in the bottom of the sixth, and that's the way things stood proceeding into the last of the ninth: the Yankees in front, 2–1, and the Dodgers without a hit. Bruce Edwards began the Dodgers' last stand with a drive toward the left-field stands that Johnny Lindell made a leaping catch of. Carl Furillo then drew a walk, the ninth surrendered by Bevens, and was run for by speedy Al Gionfriddo, who held first while Johnny Jorgenson popped out. With Pete Reiser at bat and two out, Shotton flashed the steal sign to Gionfriddo, who scampered safely into second. Bucky Harris followed with an equally controversial move by ordering an intentional walk to Reiser, thus putting the winning run on base. Eddie Miksis ran for Reiser, and Harry "Cookie" Lavagetto, in his last major-league season, pinch-hit for Eddie Stanky. Cookie swung and missed at Bevens' first pitch, then swung again at the second offering and sliced a fly ball to right that bounced off the screen and hopped away from Tommy Henrich's frantic clutches long enough for the tying and winning runs to score. The Ebbets Field crowd, silent while Bevens was working on his no-hitter, erupted joyfully as the Dodgers mobbed Lavagetto. Plate umpire Larry Goetz, momentarily befuddled by the melodramatic turnabout, started to dust off home plate after Miksis scored, then stopped and said to himself, "What am I doing? The game's over."

October 3, 1947

NEW YORK

	ab	r	h
Stirnweiss, 2b	4	1	2
Henrich, rf	5	0	1
Berra, c	4	0	0
DiMaggio, cf	2	0	0
McQuinn, 1b	4	0	1
Johnson, 3b	4	1	1
Lindell, lf	3	0	2
Rizzuto, ss	4	0	1
Bevens, p	3	0	0
Total	33	2	8

aWalked for Gregg in seventh.
bRan for Furillo in ninth.
cWalked for Casey in ninth.
dRan for Reiser in ninth.
eDoubled for Stanky in ninth.

BROOKLYN

	ab	r	h
Stanky, 2b	1	0	0
e Lavagetto	1	0	1
Reese, ss	4	0	0
Robinson, 1b	4	0	0
Walker, rf	2	0	0
Hermanski, lf	4	0	0
Edwards, c	4	0	0
Furillo, cf	3	0	0
b Gionfriddo	0	1	0
Jorgenson, 3b	2	1	0
Taylor, p	0	0	0
Gregg, p	1	0	0
a Vaughan	0	0	0
Behrman, p	0	0	0
Casey, p	0	0	0
c Reiser	0	0	0
d Miksis	0	1	0
Total	26	3	1

New York   1 0 0 1 0 0 0 0 0–2
Brooklyn   0 0 0 0 1 0 0 0 2–3

Errors—Berra, Reese, Edwards, Jorgenson. Runs batted in—DiMaggio, Lindell, Reese, Lavagetto 2. Two–base hits—Lindell, Lavagetto. Three-base hit—Johnson. Stolen bases—Rizzuto, Reese, Gionfriddo. Sacrifices—Stanky, Bevens. Double plays—Reese, Stanky and Robinson; Gregg, Reese and Robinson; Casey, Edwards and Robinson. Left on base—New York 9, Brooklyn 8. Bases on balls—Taylor 1, Gregg 3, Bevens 10. Struck out—Gregg 5, Bevens 5. Hits off—Taylor 2 in 0 (pitched to four batters), Gregg 4 in 7, Behrman 2 in 1 1/3, Casey 0 in 2/3. Wild pitch—Bevens. Winner—Casey. Loser—Bevens. Umpires—Goetz (N), McGowan (A), Pinelli (N), Rommel (A), Boyer (A), Magerkurth (N). Time—2:20. Attendance—33,443.

Eddie Miksis slides home with the winning run of the Dodgers' dramatic win over the Yankees in the fourth game of the Series. Two were out when Lavagetto came through with his pinch-hit double. Yogi Berra waits forlornly for Henrich's throw as Brooklyn players begin a victory dance. *Wide World Photos*

Hugh Casey, premier relief pitcher for the Dodgers. He led the National League in saves in 1942 and 1947, and was credited with two wins and a save in the 1947 World Series. *N.Y. Daily News Photo*

It was hard to unnerve the Yankees, however. They won the pivotal fifth game at Ebbets Field, 2–1, and returned to Yankee Stadium with a three-to-two game edge. Frank Shea went all the way in game five, knocked in a run with a single in the fourth inning, and struck out Lavagetto, pinch-hitting for Hugh Casey in the ninth. Celebrating in the clubhouse after the game, Shea said, "That three-and-two ball to Lavagetto . . . was a belt-high fast one. He never saw it. Boy, that revenge was sweet!"

One game away from elimination, the Brooks routed Allie Reynolds in the sixth game with a pair of runs in the first and third innings. The Yankees rallied to take a 5–4 lead after five innings, but the Dodgers scored four times in the top of the sixth to take an 8–5 lead. In the last of the sixth inning the Yankees got two runners on with two out, with Joe DiMaggio, the American League's Most Valuable Player in 1947, at bat. The Yankee Clipper clubbed Joe Hatten's second pitch deep toward the left-field bullpen, and the Stadium crowd roared in anticipation of a game-tying home run. But Al Gionfriddo, stationed in left for defensive purposes, sprinted to the fence, stuck out his glove, and plucked the ball off the bullpen rail. The usually imperturbable DiMaggio stopped at second, stared unbelievingly at Gionfriddo, and then disgustedly kicked the dirt.

Al Gionfriddo has just stolen a three-run homer from Joe DiMaggio in the sixth inning of the sixth World Series game. It saved the game for the Dodgers and forced a seventh contest. *UPI Photo*

Dodger hero Al Gionfriddo surrounded by admiring teammates. Reese is planting a kiss on Al's cheek, and standing, left to right, are: Dixie Walker, Bobby Bragan, and Eddie Stanky. *N.Y. Daily News Photo*

The final game matched Frank Shea and Hal Gregg, and the Dodgers scored twice in the second inning and sent Flatbush hopes soaring. The euphoria lasted until the bottom of the fourth, when hits by Bobby Brown and Tommy Henrich gave the Yankees a 3–2 lead. In the fifth Shea faltered slightly, and Joe Page took over. Page retired the next thirteen Brooklyn hitters in a row, until Eddie Miksis singled with one out in the ninth. By then the Yankees had added two insurance runs to their lead. Page got Bruce Edwards to bounce into a double play to end the game. The Yankees were 5–2 winners and World Champions.

In the boisterous Yankee clubhouse, Larry MacPhail, with tears streaming down his cheeks, shouted to everyone that he was retiring. "I'm through, I'm through! My heart won't stand it!" he ranted, waving a beer bottle and smacking his players on the back. No one took him very seriously, but it turned out he meant it. In the solemn Dodger dressing room, Burt Shotton would only say, "We'll beat the Yankees during this next ten years a whale of a lot more times than they'll beat us."

Larry MacPhail's tearful farewell after the Yankees had won the 1947 World Series. The players, whom MacPhail had tongue-lashed during the season, do not seem to share Larry's grief. Joe Page is the player nearest MacPhail, next to Page is Bobo Newsom, then Bobby Brown and Allie Reynolds. *N.Y. Daily News Photo*

CHAPTER TWO

1948

Indians, Braves, and Managerial Musical Chairs

The fact that no local team would make it into the 1948 World Series was not finally established until October 2, when the Yankees were beaten by the Boston Red Sox and eliminated from the American League pennant race. And although they were not serious contenders for most of September, the Dodgers weren't mathematically eliminated until the last week of the season.

The Boston Braves won the National League flag, for the first time since 1914. Warren Spahn and Johnny Sain were their pitching leaders, but Vernon Bickford and Bill Voiselle were considerably more helpful than the "day of rain" suggested by a writer. They combined for twenty-four victories, and each had a better ERA than Spahn.

The first play-off game in American League history was won, 8–3, by the Indians over the Red Sox at Fenway Park. Just as he had all season, Lou Boudreau, the Cleveland player-manager, led the charge. He homered twice and finished the season with 106 runs batted in and a .355 batting average. His team won the World Series, four games to two, and at the end of the year Boudreau was named the American League's Most Valuable Player.

The Dodgers won all twenty-five of their spring-training exhibition games, an accomplishment tainted somewhat when it is noted that the victories came against teams in Central America and minor-league clubs in the Southwest. Against their peers the Brooks fared less well, and as late as July 2 were in last place. At that point they rallied bravely behind the hitting of Carl Furillo and Jackie Robinson and the pitching of rookie Carl Erskine, and climbed all the way back to first place by the end of August. But six losses to the Giants during the first two weeks of September tumbled Brooklyn out of first and enabled the Braves to prevail. Retribution was exacted by the Dodgers' Rex Barney when he fired a no-hitter against the Giants—the first suffered by the

One of the finest Yankee outfields of all time: Charley "King Kong" Keller in left; Joe DiMaggio, the "Yankee Clipper," in center; and "Old Reliable" Tommy Henrich in right. They helped the Yankees capture five pennants during the 1940s. *N.Y. Daily News Photo*

The Giants' 1948 pitching staff. Left to right: Sheldon "Available" Jones, Dave Koslo, Larry Jansen, Monte Kennedy, and Clint Hartung. Jones and Jansen combined for thirty-four wins, but their mates could only total another nineteen. *UPI Photo*

Roy Campanella, in his rookie season, displays his powerful swing, which ended with his right knee nearly resting on the ground. Campy was the regular Dodger catcher for ten years.
UPI Photo

Polo Grounders in more than thirty years—but it came too late to be of any real help. The Brooks finished the season in third place, a game behind the Cardinals and seven lengths in back of the Braves.

During the 1948 season, as in 1947, Johnny Mize regularly hammered baseballs out of sight, but unlike the previous season, no one else in the Giants' lineup did except for Sid Gordon. For the second year in a row Mize shared the National League home-run title with the Pirates' Ralph Kiner, but Willard Marshall, Bobby Thomson, and Walker Cooper combined for only forty-six homers, fifty-four fewer than they had totaled in 1947. Dependable Larry Jansen had another good year with eighteen wins, and a blond-haired whippet named Carroll "Whitey" Lockman ranged impressively in left field, but the Giants ended the season in fifth place, just two games over .500. Improved defense and at least one more effective starting pitcher were needed to make the Giants contenders.

The Yankees got a big year out of Joe DiMaggio: thirty-nine homers, 155 RBIs, and a .320 average. On June 20, during a 13–2 rout of the White Sox, Joe collected a single, double, triple, two homers, and six RBIs. In two games against the St. Louis Browns in late September he smacked three homers, despite a painful charley horse, to help the Yanks gain a tie for the league lead

Above: Brooklyn-born Sid Gordon, an outfielder and third baseman for the Giants, was probably the only New York player ever given a "Day" at Ebbets Field. He is shown here with some of the gifts he received on July 3, 1948. *UPI Photo.* *Right:* Joe Hatten won fifty-six games during his first four seasons with the Dodgers, starting in 1946. He was also an effective bullpen operative. *N.Y. Daily News Photo*

with Cleveland and Boston. In the season's final games against the Red Sox, DiMaggio did all he could to stave off elimination from the pennant race. The Clipper might have won his second successive Most Valuable Player award had it not been for the brilliant play of Lou Boudreau.

The Bombers won ninety-four games, only three fewer than in 1947, but the Indians improved their 1947 performance by seventeen games in nosing out the Red Sox by a game and the Yankees by three. During August the Yankees lost a hero from their storied past when Babe Ruth succumbed to throat cancer, just a few weeks after greeting 70,000 cheering fans at Yankee Stadium's twenty-fifth anniversary celebration.

Despite its disappointing outcomes, the season was not without moment. The Dodgers, as a result of winter deals with the Braves and Pirates, shaped a starting unit that would remain substantially intact for the next ten years. Eddie Stanky was dealt to Boston, and replaced at second base by Jackie Robinson. Reserve catcher Gil Hodges moved to first, and in June a stocky slugger named Roy Campanella was brought up from St. Paul to take over the catching duties. The Pirate trade brought Preacher Roe and Billy Cox to the Dodgers, in exchange for Dixie Walker. And Walker's departure gave young

Duke Snider a chance to join regulars Gene Hermanski and Carl Furillo in the Brooklyn outfield.

The Yankees introduced Ed Lopat, Joe Collins, and Cliff Mapes into their roster at the beginning of the season, and at the end of the year announced the promotions of Hank Bauer and Gene Woodling.

The Giants had only one newcomer to warrant notice, Don Mueller, but they produced the biggest news of the season by hiring Leo Durocher away from the Dodgers. When his team started to flop in early July, Giant president Horace Stoneham concluded that easygoing Mel Ott, the manager since 1942, and a Polo Grounds idol since 1922, would have to go. Stoneham learned that Brooklyn Dodger owner Branch Rickey was disenchanted with Durocher, even though Leo had been reinstated for the 1948 season by Commissioner Chandler and had managed to stay out of trouble. Stoneham asked Rickey's permission to make Durocher an offer, Rickey agreed, Durocher agreed, and New Yorkers were stunned to learn on the morning of July 16 that popular Mel Ott had been replaced as Giant manager by Leo Durocher, who since 1940 had been the primary irritant in the hot-blooded Giant-Dodger rivalry. The confusion of loyalties was almost too much for many Giant fans. Pragmatic

Leo Durocher in his first appearance at Ebbets Field in a Giants uniform. The date is July 27, 1948, Leo's forty-fifth birthday. All of the spectators, with the notable exception of the lady in the upper left of the picture, seem amused by Leo's unfamiliar garb. *N.Y. Daily News Photo*

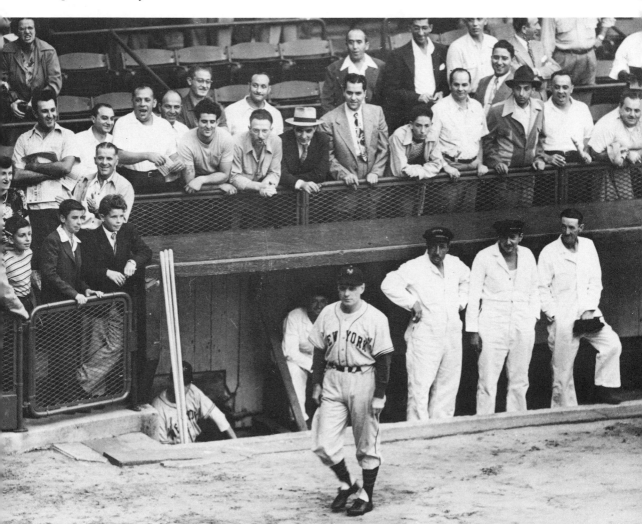

Jackie Robinson moved to second base in 1948. His slightly pigeon-toed stance is in evidence here, as he makes the force on Johnny Mize and relays the ball to first. The umpire is Frank Dascoli. *Brown Brothers*

Left: Years before Willie Mays perfected the basket catch, Giant infielder Bill Rigney delighted New York fans with it. He is seen here in a spring-training practice session. *N.Y. Daily News Photo. Right:* Bobby Brown hit .300 in 113 games for the Yankees in 1948. In seventeen World Series games he batted .439. His medical studies during the off-season earned him the inevitable nickname "Doc." *N.Y. Daily News Photo*

types felt that Leo would inject some needed vitality into the team, but the majority were convinced that Leo's presence would be poisonous. The New York *Times* interviewed a Peekskill resident named Charley Chefalo, the self-proclaimed No. 1 Giant fan, who for twenty-five years had rarely missed a Giant home game. "That settles it, brother, I'm through," said Charley. "I'll never enter the Polo Grounds again." When asked what his attitude would be if Durocher led the Giants to a pennant, Charley snorted and said, "That's impossible."

The Dodgers reactivated Burt Shotton to replace Durocher, and a number of Brooklyn players expressed relief. Neither Durocher nor Shotton managed to win a pennant, but a new era of embittered Giant-Dodger confrontations had begun.

Then the Yankees got into the act. At the end of the season they rewarded Bucky Harris for a good season with his walking papers. Throughout the season Harris had struggled for control of the team with George Weiss, the Yankee general manager, who deemed Harris's low-key manner not suggestive of decisive leadership. Almost as surprising as Durocher's move was the subsequent Yankee announcement that they had hired fifty-eight-year-old Charles Dillon "Casey" Stengel to replace Harris. In 1948 Casey managed the Oakland Oaks to the Pacific Coast League championship, and during the 1920s hit over .400 for the Giants in two World Series against the Yankees. But despite these accomplishments, he had a wisecracking, clownish image that was difficult to conceive as adapting to the stolid Yankee demeanor.

The New York press had fun ribbing Stengel's eccentric syntax and describing again the legendary pranks, but Casey let them laugh while he began shaping another Yankee dynasty.

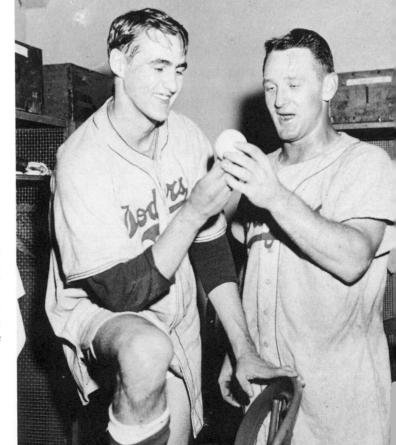

Rex Barney, on the left, and his catcher, Bruce Edwards, admire the last ball Barney used in his no-hitter over the Giants on September 9. Rex won fifteen games in 1948, but never won more than nine in his other five years with Brooklyn. *N.Y. Daily News Photo*

CHAPTER THREE

The Supporting Players

Notably rich in ballplayers, New Yorkers also possessed a wealth of gifted and colorful individuals who reported, described, and embellished the action on the field. There were six daily newspapers published in the city, plus more in the immediate suburbs, that featured the glittering by-lines of Stanley Woodward, Red Smith, Arthur Daley, Dick Young, Jimmy Cannon, and Roscoe McGowen, to name a very few. Three radio and television networks carried the voices of Red Barber, Vince Scully, Mel Allen, and Russ Hodges, plus additional personalities involved with pre- and post-game shows, re-creations, and contests for Little Leaguers. Even the organist at Ebbets Field and the public-address announcer at Yankee Stadium achieved special distinction. And the New York fan, ranging from the Brooks Brothers–suited plutocrat in a Yankee Stadium box seat to the T-shirted leather-lung in the bleachers at Ebbets Field, read, watched, and listened avidly.

Walter Lanier Barber, a descendant of the American poet Sidney Lanier, broadcast major-league baseball for thirty-three years: five with the Cincinnati Reds, fifteen in Brooklyn, and thirteen for the Yankees. Born in Columbus, Mississippi, Barber worked as an announcer for the University of Florida radio station, and made his debut as a baseball announcer in a studio where a Western Union teletype had been set up. Red described the game setting as best he could, gave the starting lineups, and then reported the action as it clicked across his desk; hit to right, hit to center, hit to left. The suspense mounted as the wire began clicking again, but to Barber's consternation, it was announcing the lead-off hitter for the home team in the bottom of the first inning. It was evident that the wire operator was an unschooled baseball observer who had described fly balls to the outfield in such a way as to indicate that the bases were loaded. Barber fled the studio in dismay and refused to return until a more experienced operator could be found. An elaborate code was subsequently devised in a further effort to prevent future embarrassments.

After his Cincinnati stint, Red arrived in Brooklyn in 1939. Two years later the Brooklyn Chamber of Commerce cited him as "the young man who has made the largest civic contribution to Brooklyn betterment." In his preface to Barber's autobiography, *Rhubarb in the Catbird Seat,* Robert Creamer describes the Red Barber magic:

> Lord, those years were exciting. Everybody talked baseball. If a million people went to Ebbets Field to see the Dodgers play, ten million listened to Red

broadcast their games. I was a Yankee fan in those days—I rooted for the Yanks when they played the Dodgers in the 1941 World Series—but I never listened to Yankee ball games. I listened to Barber and the Dodgers. Everybody did. In the summer of 1941 you did not need to own a radio to hear Red broadcast. You could walk up a street and hear the game through one open window after another and never miss a pitch. You could thread your way through the crowd on a beach and get the game from a dozen different portables. In traffic you'd hear it from a hundred different cars.

Barber's impact on New York was extraordinary. Everybody knew who Red Barber was, even my maiden aunt—literally. The language he used in his broadcasts became part of everyone's speech. James Thurber used some of it in a memorable short story that was later made into a motion picture. Much of it sounds dated now—sittin' in the catbird seat, tearin' up the pea patch, walkin' in tall cotton, we got a rhubarb growin' in the infield, the bases are FOB: full of Brooklyns—but a cliché is essentially a phrase that is so good everybody keeps repeating it. And Barber was good. Mixed in with all that southern corn were felicitous phrases like "advancing to third on the concomitant error," which flattered his ever-more-knowledgeable audience, an audience that was ever more knowledgeable primarily because of him.*

*© 1968 by W. L. Barber. Reprinted by permission.

Connie Desmond, on the right, describes the action, while his broadcasting partner, Walter "Red" Barber, pauses for a three-inning breather. Not visible is Barber's three-minute egg timer, which would remind him to give the score of the game. Red believed that no more than three minutes should elapse before listeners were reminded of the score. *Wide World Photos*

Red joined the Yankees in 1954 and stayed until his characteristic reluctance to varnish the truth ran afoul of a thin-skinned Yankee management in 1966. When he first joined the Yankees, he was told by several players that they had often tried to get home early enough from their games to listen to his Dodger broadcasts. Red considered this an ultimate tribute.

For most of his Brooklyn tenure Barber was joined by Connie Desmond and Vince Scully. The three of them formed the finest broadcasting crew in the history of the profession. Desmond joined the Dodgers in 1943, after a brief career as a professional singer and a decade of working in the Midwest handling minor-league baseball and Big Ten football. His crisp delivery and resonating voice contrasted perfectly with Barber's langourous style and slightly more tenorlike tones. Scully did broadcast work at Fordham University's campus station, then began his professional career at WTOP in Washington, D.C. Barber heard him and invited him to Brooklyn for an interview with Branch Rickey. The appointment was set for 11:00 A.M., and at 11:45 Barber's phone rang. It was Rickey, who said, "Walter, I don't wish to trespass on your time, but you have found the right young man." Barber and Rickey shared excellent taste in broadcasters. Scully is today the best in the business.

Yankee haters heaped much of their animosity on Mel Allen, who from 1939 to 1964 described the exploits of the Yankees with enthusiasm, intensity, and, at times, maddening detail. For some reason it was considered bad form for Allen to be so obviously a Yankee devotee, while at the same time no one criticized broadcasters in other cities who expressed strong home-team loyalties. Bob Prince, the Pittsburgh Pirates' play-by-play operative, was in the radio booth with Russ Hodges the day Bobby Thomson poled his historic home run. Practically speechless with excitement, Hodges handed the microphone to Prince, who pronounced the following ode to home-town pride: "Ladies and gentlemen, the Giants have won the pennant, but Ralph Kiner is still the National League home-run king." However, not so much as a spirited "How about that!" could escape Allen without his detractors whining their disapproval.

Before joining the Yankees as Arch McDonald's assistant in 1939, Mel covered a wide variety of sports, and as his Yankee duties permitted, he continued to do so. But baseball and the Yankees were his first loves, and for a quarter of a century he held forth as the official voice of the Bronx Bombers. His partners in the booth included McDonald, Russ Hodges, Curt Gowdy, Red Barber, and Phil Rizzuto, but none of them was ever so closely identified with Yankee broadcasts and telecasts.

The late Russ Hodges was an accomplished major-league broadcaster by the time he was twenty-five. For three years he handled Cubs and White Sox games, then moved to Washington in 1938, where he stayed until 1945. He worked next with Mel Allen and the Yankees for three years before joining the Giants and fulfilling his fondest professional ambition. No one who heard it will ever forget his description of the final moments of the third Giant-Dodger play-off game in 1951. His voice was tense with hopeful excitement as the Giants got men on base and Brooklyn changed pitchers, and when Thomson's drive cleared the left-field wall, he unloosed the only unabashed cheer the author has ever heard sounded by a sportscaster. Russ dutifully

The best broadcaster in the business today is Vince Scully, who got his start with the Dodgers in 1951 as an understudy to Red Barber. Vin can still be heard describing the exploits of the Dodgers, and he has become a radio and television personality in talk and game shows. *UPI Photo*

The voice of the Yankees: Mel Allen. He described the action on radio and television for more than twenty-five years, and alternately delighted and infuriated two generations of listeners and viewers. *N.Y. Daily News Photo*

Russ Hodges worked with Mel Allen for three years doing Yankee broadcasts, then joined the Giants in 1948. Few broadcasters have been with a team longer than Russ, who remained with the Giants until his death in 1971. *UPI Photo*

followed his beloved Giants to San Francisco in 1958 and remained with them until his death in 1971.

A long-time co-worker of Hodges was Ernie Harwell, who now broadcasts the Detroit Tigers games. After World War II he signed on as the broadcaster for the Atlanta Crackers and three years later was asked to come to Brooklyn and fill in for the ailing Red Barber. Barber soon recovered, and Harwell moved uptown and formed a solid partnership with Russ Hodges.

New Yorkers who missed the regular broadcasts of weekday games could tune in at 7:00 P.M. to radio station WMGM for "Today's Baseball," a thirty-minute program that re-created the games played by the local teams that afternoon. Routine events were summarized, but at decisive moments a conventional play-by-play format was simulated, complete with dramatic pauses and the swelling murmur of the crowd. The crack of the bat was produced by the announcer's rapping a wooden block beneath his microphone, an effect almost exclusively reserved for home runs, at which point the engineer would turn up the crowd-noise record full blast. It was a radio version of instant replay, and great fun to listen to even if you were fully informed of the game's outcome. The principal announcers during the show's lifetime were Bert Lee, Marty Glickman, Bert Lee, Jr., and Ward Wilson, joined at various times by Jim Gordon, Johnny Most, and Kal Ross.

Visitors to Ebbets field were treated not only to exciting baseball but to the talents of Gladys Goodding as well. Unlike most present-day stadium organists, who feel compelled to fill every pause in the action with cavalry charges, polkas, and hallelujah choruses, Gladys never played while a game proceeded except during the seventh-inning stretch and whenever a Dodger player hit a home run, when she would run her fingers up and down the keys as the hero made his tour of the bases. During her first season she once played "Three

Gladys Goodding was best known for her organ playing at Ebbets Field, but she also played in Madison Square Garden for sports events there. She started with the Dodgers in 1942 after writing team president Larry MacPhail from her home in St. Louis, asking for the job. *Wide World Photos*

Blind Mice" as the umpires took the field, but stony glares from the arbiters precluded any encores. Gladys was raised in St. Louis, where, after piano lessons, she would head for the ball park. Her love for baseball prompted her to write Dodger president Larry MacPhail for the stadium organist's job in 1940. Two years later she was hired and quickly became a merry and familiar part of the Ebbets Field scene. In succeeding years she played at sporting events in Madison Square Garden as well, thus inspiring one of the sports world's favorite trivia questions: Who was the only person to play for the Dodgers, Knicks, and Rangers in the same year?

In an interview for the July 1953 issue of *Baseball Magazine,* Gladys listed the favorite tunes of a few Dodger players: "I Wish You Were Jealous of Me," Dixie Walker; "Dark Eyes," Mickey Owen; "Indiana," Carl Erskine; "California, Here I Come," Duke Snider; "Tenderly," Jim Gilliam; "O Sole Mio," Carl Furillo; "Laura," Gil Hodges; and "My Old Kentucky Home," Peewee Reese.

Another jovial Ebbets Field personality was Francis "Happy" Felton, the rotund, 285-pound impresario of "Happy Felton's Knothole Gang." For the last seven seasons in Brooklyn, all Dodger home games were preceded by Happy's TV show, featuring interviews with Dodger stars and batting and fielding contests for Little Leaguers. The winner of the contest would return the next day for a televised chat with his favorite player.

Above: Happy Felton's Knothole Gang was a pre-game TV show wherein Felton, on the far left, would interview Dodger stars and officiate in contests for local Little League and Babe Ruth League players. Gil Hodges is shown here greeting some admiring fans. *Wide World Photos*   *Below:* Shorty Laurice, shown here with a cigar and bass drum, was the leader of the Dodgers' Sym-Phony band, which performed regularly at Brooklyn home games. Bobby Bragan is seen playing the snare drum, and Johnny Jorgenson seems to be wincing at the raucous din. *N.Y. Daily News Photo*

Felton ran away from home and joined the circus when he was seven, sold Pop Johnson's Snake Oil Elixir off the back of a medicine-show truck as a teen-ager, later worked as a vaudeville comic and violin player in the Ben Bernie orchestra, and still later wrote songs, made movies, and emceed various radio game shows. Only in Brooklyn could a man of so many parts find a suitable home.

The intimate, noisy atmosphere of the Flatbush ball yard provided an accommodating habitat for all sorts of bizarre characters. Shorty Laurice was the founder and bass-drum player of the Dodgers' Sym-Phony, an unlikely group of trombonists and percussionists who affected derelict disguises and raucously serenaded the opposition from behind the visitors' dugout. And the public-address announcer for thirty-three years was Tex Rickards, renowned for his startling slips of the tongue. "A little boy has been found lost" was one of his memorable pronouncements, as was the one he voiced after the umpires had requested him to ask the fans in the front row of the left-field grandstand to take their coats and sweaters off the railings: "The umpires request that the fans in the left-field boxes will kindly remove their clothing."

Since 1951 the more dignified environment of Yankee Stadium has been an appropriate stage for the talents of Bob Sheppard, the Yankees' public-address announcer. His professional qualifications are unimpeachable; he holds a professorship of public speaking at St. John's University, from which he graduated after earning seven varsity letters in football and baseball. After military service, Sheppard began his announcing career when he asked the promoters of an exhibition football game between the New York Yanks and the Chicago Rockets to let him handle the PA duties. This was in the late summer of 1948, shortly after Babe Ruth's death. During the half Sheppard asked the spectators to rise and observe a moment of silence for the Babe. It was a poignant moment, and Sheppard's sensitive handling of it did not go unnoticed by a

For more than twenty years the Yankee Stadium public-address announcer has been Bob Sheppard. Bob began his chores in 1951 and still works all Yankee and football Giants home games. He is also a professor of public speaking at St. John's University, where in his undergraduate days he won seven varsity letters in football and baseball.
N.Y. Yankees

Brooklyn football Dodgers executive in attendance. He invited Sheppard to handle the Dodger games at Ebbets Field, and when they folded, Sheppard moved to Yankee Stadium and worked for the football Yanks. Shortly thereafter he took on the baseball Yankees and has been at the microphone ever since. He even had a brief fling with Harry Wismer and the Titans at the Polo Grounds, thus completing a tour of duty in each of the city's major-league parks. His is a craft that is much taken for granted, but for thousands of appreciative Yankee fans a home game would not be the same without Bob Sheppard's voice ringing clearly through Yankee Stadium.

Television played an increasingly important role in the drama of New York baseball, from its fledgling status in 1947 to its highly influential position by the late 1950s. But in 1950 it was still something of a novelty, as the following article by Joe Williams indicates.

TV OR NOT TV

There is no question you get more for your money on TV. Take the first game of the World Series. The camera boys brought you the plays. To be sure you didn't miss, the voice boys followed through.

TV is probably a greater blessing to the slothful bean and the stagnant noggin than radio. I do not pretend to speak as an authority, though. I have reason to believe I am adequately equipped. My handicap lies in opportunity. Most of the time I'm at the scene of the crime myself.

Nevertheless, it is patent even from desultory contacts that any medium which presents a picture of the obvious and then explains it is not likely ever to be faulted as too subtle or esoteric.

I doubt, for instance, that anyone TViewing the duel between the Yanks' Vic Raschi—"Big Vic Raschi"—and the Phils' Jim Konstanty—"Big Jim Konstanty"—could possibly have been mistaken as to the quality of the pitching but such is TV's distrust of audience discernment, or perhaps so boundless its solicitude, that we were repeatedly reminded it was a great pitchers' battle. Not only great but "one of the greatest in the long and colorful history of the fall classic."

Hilda Chester, the archetypal Dodger fan. She would sit behind a sign proclaiming, "Hilda Is Here," and noisily rouse her heroes with whistles, cowbells, and kazoos, as well as her own formidable lung power. *N.Y. Daily News Photo*

In artistry and competence it was top hole, at that. To the extent that he had fewer weapons and was more often in trouble, Konstanty, who is as famed for relief as a five-way cold tablet, did the more heroic job. Furthermore, he made his manager's "desperation pick" look like the product of pure genius.

The 33-year-old right-hander is what is known in the trade as a junk pitcher. This is dugout contempt for the stuff he throws. A fast ball that isn't fast—a curve ball which doesn't curve, a change of pace which doesn't change. Junk or no junk, he held the Yanks to one long run which grew out of a double and two fly outs. DiMag, Berra and Mize, backbone of the Yanks' batting order, went 0 for 10. The big guys, you'll note, didn't bother him. It was young Doc Brown, most anemic Yank in the batting order (.264) who wrote the prescription which led to Konstanty's downfall—an unorthodox double which opened the fourth.

Just where this now leaves the Phils' manager in pitching prospects we in the TV audience were not told. This is an imponderable and is no doubt considered beyond our understanding. Besides there are no pictures to go with this sort of thing and without pictures we are lost. For a time yesterday, incidentally, we really were up against it. The pictures got lost. Was that a twist!! And later on the voice which explains the pictures got lost, too. It was a miracle we got through to the end. For all TV knows we may be brighter than they think. Speaking for myself, however, I trust this will not be regarded as a challenge.

As it turned out the Phils' manager had a chance to take it all with Konstanty. It wasn't as if Eddie Sawyer were conceding the first game while giving Robin Roberts, his overworked ace, vitally needed rest. How much he'll be able to get out of Konstanty in relief from here in is a question. In any case it was a good gamble. Against Raschi the Whiz Kids couldn't have won for anybody yesterday —not even if the clock had been turned back 35 years and they had Grover Cleveland Alexander going for them. The first law of the game remains unchanged. You can't win if you don't score.

TV still has shortcomings. Did you know that Gene Woodling has baby blue eyes. . . ."just like Eddie Stanky's?" When the voice let us in on that piquant secret yesterday we were made to realize what color is going to mean, how infinitely more satisfying our sports presentations will be.

This may seem a minor item but you'd be surprised how it grows on you. In the beginning I had no interest at all in the color of young Doc Brown's eyes. But after he scored and the run loomed increasingly important inning after inning the desire for this information became almost uncontrollable.

It is not enough to know that a ballplayer hits straight away, is a good glove man, carries a rifle for an arm, is the son of an immortal (Dick Sisler), was born in the shadow of Shibe Park (Del Ennis), that his favorite hobby is writing to Howdy Doody. What's the color of his eyes? Both of them. And if, like John Barrymore's they are bloodshot, let us know. We of the TV audience simply can't get enough useless information, a fact which our hosts, very sensibly, do not dispute.*

Williams was in the hospital, recovering from injuries received in a plane crash, and unable to cover a World Series game for the first time in many years.

A final note on the subject of the New York fan: No doubt an entire book could be written about him, but for the purposes of this chapter the following tirade may suffice to indicate something of his variety and temperament. It was written by a reporter for the *Sporting News,* perhaps after having spent an eventful afternoon at Ebbets Field.

Early arrivals for the first game of the 1947 World Series line up outside Yankee Stadium. Competition was fierce for choice bleacher seats, prompting many zealots to show up at the gate the night before the game. *N.Y. Daily News Photo*

I have made a study of rooters, noisemakers, pests and pleasures at baseball games. I have found the big, noisy, manly, good-natured if rough chap entirely unobjectionable, even pleasant and attractive, a distinct asset to the game. There is, on the other hand, the degenerate, the moron, the sadist who takes a degenerate pleasure in abusing, from the protection of the stands, men whom he would not dare abuse in a place where he would be subject to instant reprisal.

It is the narrow-foreheaded, mean-eyed, rabbit-toothed, receding-chinned, rat-faced fellow that makes most of the trouble. This is the fellow—you can see him in every stand—who yelps and cries nervously, who fumes, curses, whines, chews peanuts, gum, popcorn and drinks endless pop as the game proceeds. This is the real nuisance that should be mercilessly abated.

This picture was taken in a bar at the corner of Dean Street and Sixth Avenue in Brooklyn moments after the Dodgers dropped the seventh and deciding game of the 1952 World Series to the Yankees. Not until 1955 did the Dodgers improve the October dispositions of their faithful fans. *N.Y. Daily News Photo*

CHAPTER FOUR

1949

Crippled Bombers Nip Bosox at the Wire

Thomas David Henrich, for eleven years the Yankee right fielder and occasional first baseman, was also an active member of the Society for the Preservation and Encouragement of Barber Shop Quartet Singing in America. He was a steadfast family man, was never known to voice an oath stronger than "goldurn," and was often referred to as "Plain Joe Citizen" or "Strictly Massillon, Ohio." Yankee manager Casey Stengel said of him, "He's a fine judge of a fly ball. He fields grounders like an infielder. He never makes a wrong throw, and if he comes back to the hotel at three in the morning when we're on the road and says he's been sitting up with a sick friend, he's been sitting up with a sick friend."

These were not the qualities that inspired the nickname "Old Reliable," however. Throughout his career, which began with the Yankees in 1937, Henrich displayed a singular talent for producing the big play: a rally-ending catch or, more often, a game-winning hit. In 1948 he led the majors in runs scored, paced the American League with fourteen triples, and of his twenty-five home runs four were hit with the bases full.

In the first weeks of the 1949 season Tommy embellished his reputation. On opening day, with the Yankees losing to the Senators, 2–1, in the last of the ninth, he drilled a two-run homer that won the game. The next afternoon he homered again, and ten days later he hit another two-run homer in the last of the ninth that beat the Red Sox, 4–3. When the World Champion Cleveland Indians visited New York for the first time in 1949, Henrich's home run won the first game, and two more Henrich clouts the following afternoon helped the Yankees chase Bob Feller from the mound. A week later in Detroit he homered twice against the Tigers and had a game-winning run batted in.

Without Henrich's sizzling bat the Yankees, with injuries mounting and Joe DiMaggio completely sidelined until July, might have been buried in the second division by the end of June. Instead, they were in first place at that point. In the first sixty-five games of the season, Tommy Henrich supplied the game-winning hit eighteen times. He belted sixteen home runs over that stretch, twelve of which decided the outcome of a game.

The most potent Giant slugger was Leo Durocher, at least according to a particular Dodger rooter who charged that Leo had punched him at the end of a Giant-Dodger game at the Polo Grounds. Leo denied the charge, but Commissioner Chandler suspended the Giant manager, pending the results of an investigation. Charges were subsequently dropped and Durocher restored to active duty, but his players were neither amused nor inspired by Leo's adventures and plodded through another undistinguished season. Monte Irvin and Henry Thompson, the team's first black players, were called up from Jersey City in midseason, but played irregularly and contributed little. The Polo Grounders finished fifth for the second year in a row, and Durocher haters wore smug expressions.

During the 1940s and 1950s Dodger uniform No. 1 was worn by Peewee Reese, the Dodger team captain by designation and its leader by definition. He was neither a spectacular glove man nor a potent hitter, but he and Jackie Robinson formed a flawless double-play combination, and his speed and precise knowledge of the strike zone made Reese an ideal lead-off hitter. In 1949 he led the National League in runsscored with 132, walked 116 times, and stole twenty-six bases.

Reese's steady play was an important factor in the Dodgers' successful run for the 1949 pennant. Another was the home-run power of Gil Hodges, Duke Snider, and Roy Campanella. A third was the play of Jackie Robinson, who hit .342, drove in 124 runs, and was named the National League's Most

Casey Stengel's first year as Yankee manager was marked with daily perplexities. Injuries crippled his star players for most of the season, but somehow Stengel guided the team to a pennant and world championship. This picture was taken early in the season and shows Stengel, Berra, and Vic Raschi awaiting help from the bullpen. *N.Y. Daily News Photo*

During his first four seasons with the Giants, Carroll "Whitey" Lockman played left field. In this picture he has caught up with a long drive hit by Carl Furillo of the Dodgers just as it was about to scatter the denizens of the Brooklyn bullpen. *UPI Photo*

As the Dodgers battled for the 1949 pennant, the aggressive baserunning of Jackie Robinson was very much in evidence. Here he is completing a successful steal of home in classic hook-sliding, fist-clenching, and cap-flying style. His teammate Roy Campanella ducks out of the way as Cincinnati catcher Walker Cooper catches the ball too late to make the tag. *N.Y. Daily News Photo*

Valuable Player. And finally there was six-foot-four Don Newcombe, who was brought up from Montreal in May, shut out the Reds, 3–0, in his first start, pitched three straight shutouts in August, and finished with a 17–8 record.

With all this going for them, the Dodgers were still pressed to the season's final weekend by the St. Louis Cardinals. With two games left to each club—two for the Brooks in Philadelphia, and a pair for the Cardinals in Chicago—the Dodgers led by one game. The Dodgers lost their first game to the Phillies, but the Cardinals lost too and failed to gain ground. The next day the Dodgers took a 5–0 lead, only to have Newcombe falter and allow the Phils to achieve a 7–7 tie. In the top of the tenth, with the news in from Chicago that the Cardinals had won, Brooklyn scored twice on hits by Duke Snider and Luis Olmo. When Jack Banta retired the Phillies in the last of the tenth, the Dodgers were National League champs.

The injury-riddled Yankees also fought down to the season's final weekend, only they were on the short end of a one-game lead. The Boston Red Sox were in first place and on their way to New York for two games, needing to win only one to capture the flag. With all their infirmities, it was a minor miracle that the Yanks hadn't been outdistanced by Labor Day. But beginning with Henrich's early-season deeds, the Bombers produced a succession of heroics that kept them in the league lead from late April through the third week in September. At the end of June their greatest hero, Joe DiMaggio, returned to the lineup and provided the most unlikely melodrama of the season.

Out since spring training with a right heel still sore from a winter operation, DiMaggio played nine innings in the Mayor's Trophy game against the Giants on June 27, then traveled with the Yankees to take on the second-place Red Sox in Boston. By the time the three-game series was concluded, the Yanks had stretched their league lead by three games, and the Yankee Clipper had announced his return to action with a spectacular flourish.

This pitching quintet combined for eighty-one victories in 1949 and more than compensated for the numerous injuries suffered by Yankee regulars. Joe Page, who won thirteen games and saved twenty-seven, is the benevolent figure standing behind (left to right) Allie Reynolds, Tommy Byrne, Ed Lopat, and twenty-one-game winner Vic Raschi. *Brown Brothers*

The last Yankee player to wear uniform No. 5 was Joe DiMaggio. This picture was taken before the last two games of the season with the Red Sox, both of which were won by the Bombers, enabling them to capture the pennant. *N.Y. Daily News Photo*

In the opening game DiMaggio hit a home run with Phil Rizzuto on base that proved decisive in the Yankees' 5–4 win, and in the last of the ninth he raced into deep center field to glove Ted Williams' extra-base bid for the third out. The next afternoon his three-run homer helped the Bombers tie the Red Sox, 7–7, in the fifth inning, and in the eighth he homered again to give the Yankees their lead. In the third game the Yankees took a 3–2 lead into the top of the eighth. George Stirnweiss and Tommy Henrich reached base and DiMaggio came to the plate. Boston's ace Mel Parnell worked carefully but made his three-and-two pitch too good, and DiMaggio drove it to the base of the light tower atop the center-field bleachers. Even disappointed Red Sox fans stood and applauded DiMaggio as he loped around the bases.

Although Yankee injuries helped the Red Sox stay close, it was Boston's play after the All Star break that finally enabled them to overtake the Bombers. They won fifty-nine and lost nineteen during the second half of the season and, with a game advantage and two to play, they looked unbeatable. Mel Parnell and Ellis Kinder had both won twenty games, Bobby Doerr, Johnny Pesky, Dom DiMaggio, and Ted Williams were hitting over .300, and Williams and Vernon Stephens had combined for eighty-two homers and 318 RBIs.

On Saturday, October 1, the Red Sox, anxious to clinch the pennant in the first of the two-game match-up at Yankee Stadium, sent Mel Parnell to the mound, seeking his twenty-sixth victory. It was Joe DiMaggio Day, and after the gift-giving and speech-making, the Yankees took the field and quickly fell

The classic form of "Joltin' Joe" DiMaggio, in action here during the first game of the 1949 Series. It was not a particularly good Series for him, but his hitting over the last half of the season made it possible for the Yankees to remain in contention. *N.Y. Daily News Photo*

behind, 4–0. Allie Reynolds was replaced by bullpen master Joe Page, who checked the Boston attack while Yankee hitters tied the score with two runs in the fourth and two more in the fifth. The tie prevailed until the last of the eighth, and then Johnny Lindell, who had hit just five home runs in seventy-seven games, smacked reliever Joe Dobson's first pitch into the lower left-field stands to give the Yankees a 5–4 lead. Joe Page made it stand up. In his sixtieth appearance of the season he retired the Red Sox in the ninth, completing a one-hit, shutout performance over the last six and two-thirds innings. The race was tied, with one game to go, and Casey Stengel told a reporter, "I think we've got 'em. I can feel it in my bones."

Nearly 70,000 spectators crowded into Yankee Stadium to see the deciding game of the 1949 race. The Red Sox and Yankees both depended upon twenty-game-winning right-handers: Ellis Kinder and Vic Raschi. The Bombers struck first when Phil Rizzuto led off the Yankee half of the first inning with a triple, and scored on an infield out. That solitary run loomed larger as inning after inning proceeded with no further scoring. In the last of the eighth, with Kinder out for a pinch hitter and Mel Parnell on in relief, "Old Reliable" Tommy Henrich belted a homer that made the score 2–0. Then three more runs scored after two were out when rookie Jerry Coleman blooped a double down the right-field line with the bases loaded. A ninth-inning Red Sox rally fell two runs short, and the Yankees were 5–3 winners and American League champions. They had beaten one of the most potent teams ever fielded by the Boston Red Sox, and had done it with DiMaggio, Henrich, and Yogi Berra in the lineup together just fifteen times all season.

October 2, 1949

BOSTON	ab	r	h	o	a		NEW YORK	ab	r	h	o	a
D. DiMaggio, cf	4	0	0	5	0		Rizzuto, ss	4	1	2	1	7
Pesky, 3b	3	0	0	1	0		Henrich, 1b	3	1	1	10	0
Williams, lf	2	1	0	0	0		Berra, c	4	0	1	5	0
Stephens, ss	4	1	1	2	3		J. DiMaggio, cf	4	0	1	3	0
Doerr, 2b	4	1	2	0	6		Woodling, lf	0	0	0	0	0
Zarilla, rf	4	0	1	1	0		Lindell, lf	2	0	1	1	0
Goodman, 1b	3	0	1	9	1		Bauer, lf-rf	0	1	0	0	0
Tebbetts, c	4	0	0	6	0		Johnson, 3b	4	1	2	0	0
Kinder, p	2	0	0	0	2		Mapes, rf-cf	3	1	0	3	0
a Wright	0	0	0	0	0		Coleman, 2b	4	0	1	3	1
Parnell, p	0	0	0	0	0		Raschi, p	3	0	0	1	0
Hughson, p	0	0	0	0	0							
Total	30	3	5	24	12		Total	31	5	9	27	8

aWalked for Kinder in eighth.

```
Boston      0  0  0  0  0  0  0  0  3–3
New York    1  0  0  0  0  0  0  4  x–5
```

Error—Williams. Runs batted in—Henrich 2, Coleman 3, Doerr 2, Goodman. Two-base hit—Coleman. Three-base hits—Rizzuto, J. DiMaggio, Doerr. Home run—Henrich. Stolen bases—Goodman, Lindell. Double plays—Coleman and Henrich; Rizzuto and Henrich; Doerr, Stephens, and Goodman. Left on base—Boston 5, New York 6. Bases on balls—Raschi 5, Kinder 3, Hughson 1. Struck out—Raschi 4, Kinder 5. Hits off—Kinder 4 in 7, Parnell 2 in 0, Hughson 3 in 1. Wild pitch—Raschi. Passed ball—Berra. Winner—Raschi. Loser—Kinder. Umpires—Hubbard, Rommel, Berry, Summers, Honochick, and Hurley. Time—2:30. Attendance—68,055.

The World Series was won by the Yankees with an abruptness that stunned the Dodgers and their fans. The Brooks went into the 1949 Series with hot hitters, a pitching staff that had led the league in strikeouts and shutouts, and a strong feeling that the better team had lost the 1947 Series. Five days later they were incontestably whipped.

The opener at Yankee Stadium matched seventeen-game winner Allie Reynolds and Brooklyn's fireballing rookie Don Newcombe. In nine innings Reynolds allowed two hits, no runs, and struck out nine batters. In eight innings Newcombe gave up five hits, no runs, and fanned eleven. This classic duel was

National League Rookie of the Year in 1949, Don Newcombe won seventeen games and started the first game of the 1949 World Series for the Dodgers. He pitched brilliantly, but one swing of Tommy Henrich's bat ruined his dream. *UPI Photo*

Tommy Henrich, Roy Campanella, and the plate umpire watch as Henrich's drive speeds toward the right-field stands and brings the first game of the Series to an abrupt end. *N.Y. Daily News Photo*

ended by Tommy Henrich, the first batter in the last of the ninth. He connected with a 2–0 curve ball, and Yankee fans shot to their feet and roared as the ball soared ten rows deep into the right-field stands. Newcombe never turned around. The crack of the bat and the crowd's response told him the game was over. As Newk trudged wearily toward his dugout, Allie Reynolds was whispering to himself, "Allie, old boy, it's all over. You don't have to go out there again."

Spidery Preacher Roe spun a 1–0 shutout the next day to get the Dodgers even. Vic Raschi pitched well for the Yankees but was not quite equal to Roe's beguiling assortment of curves, change-ups, and moistened fast balls. In the second inning a double by Jackie Robinson, followed by Gil Hodges' single, gave the Preacher the only run he needed. But in the fourth inning a hard grounder hit by Johnny Lindell injured his right hand. Roe finished the game but would not appear again in the Series.

Midway through the season the Yankees picked up Johnny Mize from the Giants. It was reported that Leo Durocher had become disenchanted with Mize and had concluded that the big slugger was too old and too slow to perform usefully. Mize's first appearance in a World Series came in the top of the ninth inning of the third 1949 Series contest, with the score tied, 1–1, and the bases loaded. The Dodger bench, aware that Leo Durocher was watching the game from a third-base box seat, chanted, "Leo's watching you! Leo's

Henrich is greeted at home plate by a Yankee Stadium attendant, Yogi Berra, coach Bill Dickey, and the bat boy. Don Newcombe can be seen trudging into the Dodger dugout, a 1–0 loser on a home run in the last of the ninth inning. It was the first of many World Series setbacks for the big man. *Wide World Photos*

On the left is Preacher Roe, giving some advice to Ralph Branca. Roe shut out the Yankees, 1–0, in the second game of the 1949 Series, and Branca nearly duplicated the feat in the third game, until Johnny Mize's pinch hit in the ninth inning wrecked the Dodgers. *N.Y. Daily News Photo*

watching you!" as Mize dug in against Ralph Branca. The taunts had barely died out when Mize lined a long single off the Ebbets Field right-field screen. Two runs scored, and a runner advanced to third and scored moments later on Jerry Coleman's single. Luis Olmo and Roy Campanella hit bases-empty homers in the last of the ninth to get the Dodgers back to 4–3, but Joe Page, who had given up only three hits since relieving Tommy Byrne in the fourth, retired the Brooks with no further damage.

The fourth game, played again at Ebbets Field, went to the Bombers, 6–4. Don Newcombe, working with only two days' rest, was routed in the fourth inning, and Allie Reynolds relieved Ed Lopat in the sixth after the Dodgers had reached the Junkman for seven singles and four runs. Allie retired the last ten Brooklyn hitters in a row, five on strikeouts.

And suddenly Burt Shotton was out of pitchers. Preacher Roe was injured, and Newcombe and Branca were spent. Six remnant hurlers pitched, flinched, and ducked as the Yankees racked up a 10–1 lead going into the last of the sixth. The Dodgers made the score respectable by scoring once in the sixth and four times in the seventh, but the latter outburst only succeeded in alerting Joe Page, who came on and blanked the Dodgers the rest of the way. It was the first of seven world championships for Casey Stengel, who analyzed his success by stating, "I am the same kind of a manager I always was, but nowadays I seem to get a little more assistance from my help."

It is the ninth inning, the score is tied, 1–1, there are two outs, and Johnny Mize has just hit a ball off the right-field screen that has Yogi Berra and Bobby Brown scampering for home. Frank Crosetti is the Yankee third-base coach waving the runners home, while Branca and his teammates watch helplessly. *Wide World Photos*

Yankee heroes celebrate in the clubhouse after their third-game Series victory. Johnny Mize is on the left, Joe Page, who pitched the last five and two-thirds innings to gain the victory, is next to Mize, and on the right is young Jerry Coleman, who scored the fourth run in the 4–3 Yankee win. *N.Y. Daily News Photo*

CHAPTER FIVE

1950

Yankees Bury Whiz Kids

After thirteen seasons of futility, during which they escaped the second division only three times, the Giants developed into legitimate contenders in the second half of the 1950 season. Since taking over as manager in 1948, Leo Durocher had been saying that "my kind of team" would be needed to win a pennant. Leo's preferences did not include a reliability on home-run sluggers who were also indifferent fielders and shambling base runners. Walker Cooper went to the Reds, Johnny Mize was sold to the Yankees, and prior to the 1950 season Willard Marshall and Sid Gordon were traded to the Boston Braves for Alvin Dark and Eddie Stanky. Dark was a smooth-fielding shortstop who had hit .322 for the pennant-winning Braves in 1948, and Stanky was just the sort of gritty performer Durocher admired: always hustling and devising new ways to win ball games. Strength up the middle was fortified by the fleet Bobby Thomson in center field and catcher Wes Westrum, who made just one error in 139 games. Home runs flew with less frequency, but the team's fielding average was the second best in the league, and Dark and Stanky finished close behind Reese and Robinson in double-play production.

Speed and defense were not the only factors in the Giants' improvement, however. The pitching staff received a tremendous boost with the addition of Jim Hearn and the return of Salvatore Anthony Maglie from exile. Hearn was a bargain. Picked up on waivers from the Cardinals in June, he won eleven straight games, including five shutouts, and finished with an ERA of 2.49, the best in the majors. But Maglie made the biggest difference. After appearing in thirteen games for the Giants in 1945, he joined several major-leaguers who jumped to the free-spending Mexican League the following year. Happy Chandler declared them outlaws and for several seasons barred them from returning to the majors, but in 1950 the restriction was lifted. Maglie showed up at the Giants' training camp in Tucson, failed to attract much notice, was nearly traded, and spent the early weeks of the season in the bullpen. He didn't start a game until late June, was hit hard by the Reds, and then returned to the bullpen for another month. In July he started and won an eleven-inning game against the Cardinals. His performance was worthy enough to prompt Stan Musial to ask Giant broadcaster Russ Hodges, "Where have you been keeping that guy? He's got the best curve ball I've ever seen."

Left: Gene Hermanski, one of the best of the left fielders that came and went during the 1940s and 1950s. Gene hit .298 in 1950, and was especially helpful during the Dodgers' late-summer streak that nearly overtook the Phillies. *N.Y. Daily News Photo* *Right:* Another occasional left fielder was George "Shotgun" Shuba, a natural hitter who hit nearly .400 in the minors before Brooklyn called him up. He was the second player in World Series history to hit a pinch homer, off Allie Reynolds in 1953. *N.Y. Daily News Photo*

The fortunes of the Giants began to improve in 1950, owing largely to the efforts of the players shown in the next four photos. Pictured here are Alvin Dark, throwing to first, and Eddie Stanky, a double-play combination acquired from the Boston Braves. Sam Jethroe is the runner. *UPI Photo*

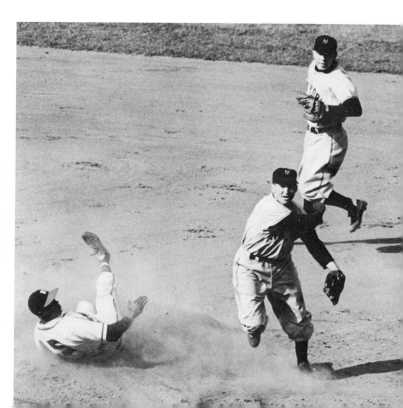

The Giant outfield comprised Whitey Lockman, on the left, in left field, Bobby Thomson in center, and Don Mueller in right field. Their average age in 1950 was twenty-four, and they quickly established themselves as Polo Grounds favorites. *UPI Photo*

Crafty Sal Maglie, after his Mexican League junket, won eighteen games for the Giants in 1950 and had an ERA of 2.71. His curve broke like a ball falling off a table, and he allowed an average of just 2.3 walks per nine innings. *Wide World Photos*

During his Mexican stint Maglie developed a curve that would tie National League hitters in knots for the next seven seasons. He also had an adequate fast ball, good control, unflappable poise, and hard-earned savvy. Best of all, he was cut from the same cloth as Durocher and Stanky: fiercely competitive and not averse to a little intimidation. Even before he threw the ball, he presented a menacing prospect. He was lean and slump-shouldered, and his shadowy beard stubble and baleful scowl created an impression of imminent calamity. Opposing hitters were made to feel that just by entering the batter's box they had done Maglie some terrible wrong.

As had Hearn, Maglie won eleven straight games during the second half of the season, and finished with an 18–4 record and the third best ERA in the majors. During his succession of victories he pitched forty-five consecutive scoreless innings, before a 258-foot homer by Gus Bell of the Reds snapped the streak just four outs short of Carl Hubbell's major-league record.

From July 20 through Labor Day the Giants played at a 34–12 clip. They finished the season in third place, their best placement since 1942, only five games behind the pennant-winning Philadelphia Phillies. A combination of youth, experience, and aggressiveness had finally created "Leo's kind of team."

Left: Another Giant with masterly control was Larry Jansen. He gave up fewer than two walks per nine innings pitched in 1950, finished third in league strikeout totals, had twenty-one complete games, and won nineteen. *UPI Photo*   *Right:* Preacher Roe won forty-one games and lost only fourteen in 1950 and 1951. He pitched for the Pirates for four seasons and once said of his former teammates, "The outfielders was like statues, and the first baseman and second baseman was like goalposts. They never seemed to get closer together as the balls bounced through." *UPI Photo*

Meanwhile, in the Bronx the rich were getting richer. Hank Bauer, Gene Woodling, and Jerry Coleman were developing into blue-chip performers, and in July the pitching staff, already affluent with the likes of Vic Raschi, Allie Reynolds, Ed Lopat, and Tommy Byrne, appreciated substantially with the addition of a baby-faced, twenty-one-year-old southpaw named Ed Ford. Ford had a quick, fluid motion, a crackling curve ball, and the cool presence of a ten-year veteran. He won his first start, 4–3, over the Detroit Tigers, and then captured eight more victories in a row, all in the heat of a contested pennant race. For despite their wealth of talent, the Yankees were led through most of the season by the Tigers, who boasted the talents of George Kell, Vic Wertz, and Hoot Evers, and Art Houtteman, Fred Hutchinson, and Hal Newhouser.

The Bombers began the season hilariously, beating the Red Sox, 15–10, at Fenway Park, after the Sox had held a 9–0 lead in the fifth inning and a 10–4 advantage as late as the eighth. The Yanks won nine in a row in May, but lost the league lead to the Tigers in June, who held it tenaciously until the middle of September. At that point Raschi and Ford helped the Yankees win two out of three games in Detroit. The Yanks went on from there to clinch the pennant when the Tigers dropped a three-game series in Cleveland.

To be sure, the Yankees had hitting and pitching, but they also had Phil Rizzuto, who enjoyed his best season in 1950. He played in every game, had two hundred hits and a .324 batting average, led the league's shortstops in fielding percentage for the second year in a row, and was named the American League's Most Valuable Player. But his value to the team transcended statistics, as impressive as the statistics were. He was a deft bunter, a reliable hit-and-run man, an alert base runner, and a steely competitor. He was a source of much delight to his manager, Casey Stengel, who said of his shortstop, "He's got that extra somethin' which you can't blame me for."

The American League's Most Valuable Player in 1950 was Phil Rizzuto, the brilliant Yankee shortstop. His .324 batting average was sixth best in the league, and for the second year in a row he had the league's best fielding average. In the long history of the Yankees no other shortstop can compare with Rizzuto. *N.Y. Daily News Photo*

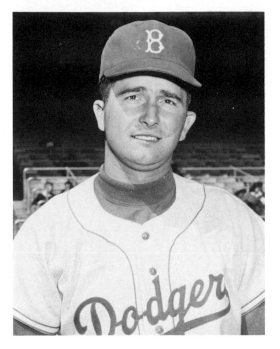

Erv Palica had his best year in 1950 with a 13–8 record. Ten of those wins came in the Dodger stretch run that came within a game of edging out the Phillies for the pennant, but in his next five years in the majors he managed to win only fourteen games. *N.Y. Daily News Photo*

On September 19 the Philadelphia Phillies were safely lodged in first place, nine games ahead of the Dodgers, and looking ahead to the World Series. Ten days later the lead had dwindled to two, partly as a result of two doubleheader losses to the Giants, and the once exuberant Whiz Kids were a rattled crew in danger of blowing one of the biggest September leads in the history of baseball. The gratified Dodgers, who had performed during 1950 somewhat less purposefully than the year before, played host to the Phillies for the last two games of the season, confident of a sweep that would force a pennant play-off. They came within inches of achieving it. A home run by Roy Campanella in the eighth inning of the first game helped Erv Palica to a 7–3 victory and the Dodgers to within a game of the lead. A Philadelphia sportswriter began his account of the contest by referring to the faltering Phils as "Fizz Kids."

The final game of the season matched the teams' aces, Robin Roberts and Don Newcombe, who had faced each other on opening day and since then had each won nineteen games. For eight innings they dueled with a run apiece. Newcombe retired the Phillies in the top of the ninth, and in the bottom of the inning the Dodgers moved Cal Abrams to second with nobody out and Duke Snider up. The Ebbets Field crowd cut loose with a raucous yell as Snider lined a single to center and Abrams scampered around third. Abrams never made it across the plate. The Phillies' center fielder, Richie Ashburn, fielded Snider's hit on the run and threw a strike to catcher Andy Seminick in plenty of time for Seminick to block the plate and tag Abrams out. It was a decisive play. The Dodgers went on to load the bases, but Roberts bore down and got the third out, and then in the top of the tenth Dick Sisler slammed a homer into the lower deck in left field that proved to be the pennant winner. The Phillies had won only three of their last twelve games, and their locker-room celebrations were dampened some by thoughts of their near catastrophe.

Steady Eddie Lopat, seen here in the third game of the 1950 World Series, was called the "Junkman," because his repertoire of pitches ranged from slow to slower to slowest, but he had pinpoint control and was especially effective in crucial games. *N.Y. Daily News Photo*

Philadelphia's luck ran out against the Yankees in the World Series. All four games were close, but it seemed that the Yankees were content to score only as many runs as were needed and leave it at that. They brushed aside the poor Phillies with lordly disdain.

In the opener, played at Shibe Park, Philadelphia manager Eddie Sawyer caused some excitement by naming Jim Konstanty as the starting pitcher. During the regular season Konstanty was the majors' top relief pitcher, having appeared in seventy-four games, winning sixteen, saving twenty-two, and recording a 2.66 ERA. Sawyer's decision was more a matter of necessity than an attempt to throw the opposition off balance. Roberts had pitched only two days earlier, seventeen-game winner Curt Simmons was in the Army, and the remaining candidates were of lesser stature.

Konstanty pitched brilliantly, but his adversary, twenty-one-game winner Vic Raschi, was nearly perfect. The Yankees got four hits and one run, and scored in the fourth on a double by Bobby Brown and two long fly balls, while Raschi was allowing just two singles and a walk.

Robin Roberts was ready for the second game, and he drew another powerful right-hander, Allie Reynolds, as his mound opponent. The Yanks got a run in the second on a walk and two singles, and in the fifth the Phils tied it up on two singles and a sacrifice fly. The score remained tied through the ninth, and then in the top of the tenth Joe DiMaggio, who had hit nearly .400 during the last two months of the season, hammered a Roberts fast ball into the seats. Reynolds was untouchable in the last of the tenth, and with a 2–1 win the Yankees were on their way to Yankee Stadium with a commanding Series lead. Asked to comment on the game, Reynolds said, "God bless Joe DiMaggio! If he hadn't hit it, I'd probably still be pitching."

The Phils came close again in the third game, and even held a 2–1 lead in the last of the eighth, but after retiring the first two hitters, starter Kenny Heintzelman walked the bases full and then watched the tying run cross when shortstop Granny Hamner booted a routine grounder. In the last of the ninth, again with two out, the Yankees' efficient if unspectacular attack produced the winning run on three timid singles, the last delivered by Jerry Coleman.

Rookie Whitey Ford, in his first World Series start, was the grateful recipient of a suddenly aroused Bomber offensive in the fourth and final game. Solid hits by Gene Woodling, Yogi Berra, and Joe DiMaggio provided two runs in the first inning, and Berra's homer and a triple by Bobby Brown accounted for three more in the sixth. Ford worked smoothly into the ninth and got two out, at which point Willie "Puddinhead" Jones singled and Del Ennis got in the way of a curve ball. The next batter, Andy Seminick, lifted a high fly to left, which Gene Woodling ran back under uncertainly and then lost in the sun. The ball bounced off the heel of his glove, and two runs scored. When Mike Goliat followed that with a single, Stengel waved in Reynolds to replace Ford, much to the displeasure of the spectators, who had been pulling for the youngster to finish. Reynolds fanned pinch hitter Stan Lopata, and the Series was abruptly over.

Casey Stengel was rewarded with a new two-year contract shortly after the Series. Shortly after that Whitey Ford reported to the Army, and American League contenders breathed a small sigh of relief.

Yankee rookie Whitey Ford had a shutout working in the ninth inning of the fourth Series game against the Phillies, until left fielder Gene Woodling misjudged and dropped a fly ball hit by Andy Seminick that allowed two runs to score. The October sun in Yankee Stadium could be murderous, as evidenced by the Phillies' bullpen operative's having to shade his eyes from the glare. *N.Y. Daily News Photo*

CHAPTER SIX

1951

Mickey, Willie, and the Little Miracle of Coogan's Bluff

Mantle and Mays arrived just in time. The last link to the superstars of the 1930s, Joe DiMaggio, was thought to be playing his last season in 1951, and the city would soon need new idols. Although it is fair to say that neither Mickey nor Willie had an outstanding rookie season, each displayed such precocious talent that by the end of the year no description of their futures sounded exaggerated.

Mantle led his Class C Joplin team to the Western Association championship in 1950, batting .383 and driving in 136 runs. He accompanied the Yankees on their last road trip in 1950, and reported to the Bomber training camp the following March. The Yankee management was planning to promote him to Kansas City, at the Triple A level, in 1951, but Mickey immediately began to explode pulverizing line drives during spring-training games, and was timed once running from home to first in a fraction over three seconds. He hit booming home runs both right-handed and left, and the accounts of his deeds relayed back to area newspapers were extravagant. Arriving in a storm of publicity, Mantle whacked a homer over the Ebbets Field scoreboard during an exhibition game with the Dodgers just before the season began. Mickey hit .402 during spring training and made the varsity.

Where to play him became an embarrassment of riches quandary. Mantle was a shortstop then, but not likely to displace Phil Rizzuto. It was decided to try him in right field, and with the help of DiMaggio and Tommy Henrich, Mickey steadily developed adequate skills in the new position. On opening day against the Red Sox at Yankee Stadium he was understandably jittery. There he was, a teen-ager, thinking to himself, "This is where Babe Ruth used to play." He looked around and saw Joe DiMaggio next to him, Phil Rizzuto at shortstop, and Vic Raschi on the mound. "I must be pretty good to be playing with these guys," he thought. He singled, drove in a run, and handled three outfield chances in his first game, and hit his first homer two weeks later against the Chicago White Sox. That same afternoon he ran from first to third on a teammate's base hit so swiftly that Stengel said after blinking twice, "He musta went through the pitcher's box."

Moods were not so buoyant at the Polo Grounds. With hopes for 1951 built on the team's fine play in the second half of the 1950 season, the Giants lost eleven straight games in April and by the end of the month were in last place. Arthur Daley, in his New York *Times* column, wrote, "It will take a miracle for the Giants to win the championship now."

A phenomenon, at least, was not long in arriving. Willie Mays was in a movie theater in Sioux City on May 12 when a message flashed on the screen: "Willie Mays—call your hotel." At that point Willie was hitting .477 for the Giants' Minneapolis farm team. Three days later he was in Philadelphia and playing center field for the Giants. He went hitless in twelve tries against the Phillies and betrayed some lack of confidence, but Durocher kept him in the lineup when the Giants returned to the Polo Grounds for a three-game series with the Boston Braves. In the opening game Willie got his first major-league hit, a towering home run off Warren Spahn that landed on the left-field grandstand roof. The authority of that blast, and the suddenness with which it disappeared, electrified the crowd. They stood and cheered their new star as he bounded across the plate.

In the spring of 1951 the greatest center fielder in Yankee history, Joe DiMaggio, was a thirty-six-year-old veteran, and Mickey Mantle a highly touted rookie of nineteen. Mickey had played shortstop in the minors but, in deference to Phil Rizzuto, was switched to the outfield when he joined the Yankees. A year later the Clipper had retired and Mickey was the regular center fielder for the next fifteen seasons. *N.Y. Daily News Photo*

Willie immediately lifted his teammates' spirits as well as those of disgruntled Giant fans. His unabashed love for the game was infectious. He played more like a schoolboy at recess than an adult earning a living. He ran like a deer, and usually left his cap fluttering behind as he rounded a bag or slid, sometimes headfirst, into a base. His throws were ground-hugging streaks that bounced perfectly into the grasp of a waiting teammate. He caught fly balls with his hands cupped nonchalantly at his waist. And his powerful swing, tautly coiled while the pitcher wound up, lashed out at pitched balls with all the deadly effect of a cobra striking. As Willie Mays gained confidence, the Giants began a slow journey back into contention.

Unfortunately for the Giants, the league-leading Dodgers were running away with the pennant. During the preceding winter Branch Rickey had sold his share of the Dodgers and Walter O'Malley had taken control. Rickey's old friend Burt Shotton was replaced by Charlie Dressen, who had once been a coach with the Yankees as well as the Dodgers. The Brooks performed well under Dressen and by midseason seemed to have everything under control. Campanella, Hodges, and Snider were hitting, and the pitching staff, paced by Preacher Roe and Don Newcombe, was well balanced and deep. On August 11 the Dodgers led the second-place Giants by thirteen and a half games.

The turning point in the extraordinary 1951 race came four days later. The Dodgers were at the Polo Grounds and losing, 3–1, as they came to bat in the eighth. Billy Cox reached base, and moved to third with one out and Carl Furillo up. Furillo belted a high drive to deep right center that looked good for extra bases but, even if caught, certain to score Cox. Racing to his left and

Willie Mays. Nineteen fifty-one was Willie's rookie year in the majors, and he is seen here in the opening game of the World Series at Yankee Stadium. He had speed and power and a joyous enthusiasm for the game that made his every move exciting to watch. *UPI Photo*

Dodger manager Chuck Dressen congratulates a weary Jackie Robinson after Jackie's game-saving catch and game-winning home run against the Phillies enabled the Dodgers to finish in a tie with the Giants for the National League flag. *N.Y. Daily News Photo*

away from the plate, Willie Mays not only caught the ball but in the same motion whirled completely around and rifled it back to the plate, where catcher Wes Westrum had time to tag out an astonished Billy Cox. The rally was nipped and the Giants held on to win. They beat the Dodgers again the next afternoon and did not lose another game until August 28. Their sixteen-game winning streak whittled the once invulnerable Dodger lead down to five games. In September "the Creeping Terror," as the Giants liked to call their pennant drive, inched closer and closer to the beleaguered Dodgers, who were trying to play not only while looking over their shoulders but also without the services of injured Roy Campanella, and with Snider, Hodges, and Furillo all fighting batting slumps. Playing .800 ball since mid-August, the Polo Grounders cut the Brooklyn lead to four games, three, two and a half, and then on September 25 they beat the Phillies for their thirty-fourth win in forty-one games. Three days later the race was tied with two games left for each club.

The drama of the National League contention overshadowed the almost equally exciting American League race. The Yankees, Indians, Red Sox, and White Sox all had turns in first place before September, when New York and Cleveland began to pull away. On September 16 the Indians were in New York for two games, leading the Yanks by one. The Bombers tied for the lead when they beat the Tribe and twenty-two-game winner Bob Feller in the opening game. The second contest went into the last of the ninth tied, 1–1. Joe DiMaggio led off with a scratch single and advanced to third on a single by Gene Woodling, and after Bobby Brown walked, Phil Rizzuto came to the plate and Cleveland third baseman Al Rosen asked DiMaggio if he thought Rizzuto

Allie Reynolds' second no-hitter of 1951 was achieved after Ted Williams popped this pitch into the mitt of Yogi Berra. Yogi had dropped a similar pop-up by Williams just seconds earlier. *Brown Brothers*

would bunt. Joe replied, "I won't say, but if he does, you'll have no chance." On Bob Lemon's second pitch, DiMaggio broke for the plate and Rizzuto squared around and dropped a perfect bunt fifteen feet in front of the plate. By the time Lemon got to the ball, DiMaggio had scored the winning run and the Yankees were in first place to stay. The actual pennant clincher came on September 28, when the Yanks swept a doubleheader from the Red Sox at Yankee Stadium. In the first game Allie Reynolds pitched his second no-hitter of the season. His first, on July 12, was recorded over the Indians, 1–0. Gene Woodling's homer accounted for the only run off Bob Feller, who had pitched his third career no-hitter just a few days earlier. Reynolds' second masterpiece was achieved after some anxious moments in the ninth inning. With two out, Ted Williams lifted a high pop to the right of home plate that Yogi Berra misjudged, lunged for, and dropped. Reynolds must have groaned right along with the many thousands who hated to see Williams get another cut. But Allie blazed away with a high fast ball, Williams popped it up again, and this time Yogi didn't miss. The Yankees had two days to rest for the World Series.

Those two days stretched to five as the Giants and Dodgers staged the most engrossing pennant climax in the history of the game. On the next to the last day of the regular season the Giants beat the Braves in Boston, and the Dodgers shut out the Phillies. The race was still tied. The next afternoon the Giants beat the Braves again, on Larry Jansen's twenty-second win. As the Giants left the field the scoreboard showed the Phillies leading the Dodgers,

8–5, in the seventh inning. On the train back to New York, with champagne cooling in the club car, the Giants learned to their dismay that the Dodgers had rallied to beat the Phils, 9–8, on Jackie Robinson's homer in the fourteenth, after a Brooklyn outburst in the eighth had tied the score and Robinson's sprawling catch of Eddie Waitkus' line drive had ended a Philadelphia winning bid in the last of the twelfth. It meant that a best-two-out-of-three-game play-off would be necessary to decide the pennant.

Robert Brown Thomson was born in Glasgow, Scotland, and came to America at the age of three. He grew up on Staten Island, was an outstanding baseball player in high school, and tried out for the Dodgers in 1942. Brooklyn dismissed him quickly, but the Giants took a chance, signed him, and sent him to their Class D team in the Appalachian League. He played poorly and spent the next three years in the Army Air Corps. In 1946 he played well enough for Jersey City to earn a trial with the Giants at the end of the season. He hit .315 in eighteen games and was up to stay. An infielder up to that time, Thomson was moved to center field, where he played for the next four and a half years. He hit with power and had good speed and range, but the arrival of Willie Mays shunted Bobby back to the infield halfway through the 1951 season. He was the regular third baseman as the play-off began in Brooklyn.

In the opening game Jim Hearn beat the Dodgers, 3–1. Andy Pafko started the scoring with a homer in the second inning, but Thomson hit a two-run homer in the fourth, and Monte Irvin homered with the bases empty in the

The first game of the best-two-out-of-three play-off for the National League pennant in 1951 was played at Ebbets Field and won by the Giants, 3–1. Bobby Thomson hit a two-run homer in the fourth and is seen here rounding third and receiving the glad hand from his third-base coach and manager Leo Durocher. Billy Cox is the Dodger third baseman. *Wide World Photos*

Jim Hearn was the winning pitcher in the first play-off game with the Dodgers. He is seen here flanked by Bobby Thomson and Monte Irvin. The second game was won by the Dodgers, setting the stage for one of the most breathtaking moments in the history of sports. *Brown Brothers*

eighth. The second and third games were set for the Polo Grounds, and a Dodger homer barrage evened the play-off with a second-game 10–0 victory.

That rout seemed to give the Dodgers enough momentum to finally finish the Giants off. In the final game they took a 4–1 lead into the last of the ninth, and with Don Newcombe getting stronger as the game progressed, Giant prospects were as dim as the leaden October sky. But Alvin Dark began the inning with a bouncing single between Robinson and Hodges, and Don Mueller followed with another bouncer through the hole that Hodges might have reached had he not been holding Dark on. As Monte Irvin stepped in, the Dodger bullpen scurried into action. Irvin popped out to Hodges, for the first and last out Newcombe was to get in the ninth. Whitey Lockman then ripped a double into the left center-field gap that scored Dark and sent Mueller skidding into third. Mueller twisted his ankle badly on the play, and as he was carried from the field, Dressen brought on Ralph Branca to pitch to Bobby Thomson. Up in the WMCA radio booth, Giant broadcaster Russ Hodges described the next ninety seconds to a transfixed listening audience:

> Bobby Thomson up there swinging. . . . He's had two out of three, a single and a double, and Billy Cox is playing him right on the third-base line. . . . One out, last of the ninth. . . . Branca pitches and Bobby takes a strike call on the inside corner. . . . Bobby hitting at .292. . . . He's had a single and a double and he drove in the Giants' first run with a long fly to center. . . . Brooklyn leads it, 4–2. . . . Hartung down the line at third not taking any chances. . . . Lockman without too big of a lead at second, but he'll be running like the wind if Thomson hits one. . . . Branca throws. . . . THERE'S A LONG DRIVE. . . . IT'S GONNA BE, I BELIEVE. . . . THE GIANTS WIN THE PENNANT! THE GIANTS WIN THE PENNANT! THE GIANTS WIN THE PENNANT! . . . BOBBY THOMSON HITS INTO THE LOWER DECK OF THE LEFT-FIELD STANDS. . . . THE GIANTS WIN THE PENNANT AND THEY'RE GOING CRAZY! . . . YAAAAAYHO!!

Absolute pandemonium ensued. Shrieking spectators spilled out of the grandstand, Eddie Stanky tackled Leo Durocher before Leo could join the welcoming mob at home plate, Thomson leaped and waved his arms as he rounded the bases, and everyone within radio and TV range observed similar hysterics. Ralph Branca and his teammates turned and moved toward the distant clubhouse—all except Jackie Robinson, who stood at his position and made sure Thomson touched every base.

Above: **The third play-off game and the 1951 National League pennant were decided by Bobby Thomson's last-of-the-ninth-inning home run that beat the Dodgers, 5–4. The hero is seen here surrounded by his exulting teammates, including the on-deck hitter, No. 24, Willie Mays.** *UPI Photo* *Below:* **The triumphant scene photographed from a center-field camera. The unlucky Brooklyn hurler, Ralph Branca, is moving dejectedly toward the clubhouse, but Jackie Robinson, defiant to the end, is standing with hands on hips and watching to make sure Thomson touches home plate.** *UPI Photo*

A delirious throng of Giant rooters stood outside the Polo Grounds clubhouse for an hour, shouting for a glimpse of their heroes. Bobby Thomson waves to the crowd, while a particularly ardent fan is gently restrained by a New York patrolman. *N.Y. Daily News Photo*

October 3, 1951

BROOKLYN	ab	r	h	o	a
Furillo, rf	5	0	0	0	0
Reese, ss	4	2	1	2	5
Snider, cf	3	1	2	1	0
Robinson, 2b	2	1	1	3	2
Pafko, lf	4	0	1	4	1
Hodges, 1b	4	0	0	11	1
Cox, 3b	4	0	2	1	3
Walker, c	4	0	1	2	0
Newcombe, p	4	0	0	1	1
Branca, p	0	0	0	0	0
Total	34	4	8	ˣ25	13

NEW YORK	ab	r	h	o	a
Stanky, 2b	4	0	0	0	4
Dark, ss	4	1	1	2	2
Mueller, rf	4	0	1	0	0
ᶜHartung	0	1	0	0	0
Irvin, lf	4	1	1	1	0
Lockman, 1b	3	1	2	11	1
Thomson, 3b	4	1	3	4	1
Mays, cf	3	0	0	1	0
Westrum, c	0	0	0	7	1
ᵃRigney	1	0	0	0	0
Noble, c	0	0	0	0	0
Maglie, p	2	0	0	1	2
ᵇThompson	1	0	0	0	0
Jansen, p	0	0	0	0	0
Total	30	5	8	27	11

ᵃStruck out for Westrum in eighth.
ᵇGrounded out for Maglie in eighth.
ᶜRan for Mueller in ninth.
ˣOne out when winning run scored.

Brooklyn	1	0	0	0	0	0	0	3	0–4	
New York	0	0	0	0	0	0	1	0	4–5	

Errors—None. Runs batted in—Robinson, Thomson 4, Pafko, Cox, Lockman. Two-base hits—Thomson, Irvin, Lockman. Home run—Thomson. Sacrifice—Lockman. Double plays—Cox, Robinson and Hodges; Reese, Robinson and Hodges. Left on bases—Brooklyn 7, New York 3. Bases on balls—Maglie 4, Newcombe 2. Struck out—Maglie 6, Newcombe 2. Hits off—Maglie 8 in 8, Jansen 0 in 1, Newcombe 7 in 8 1/3, Branca 1 in 0. Wild pitch—Maglie. Winner—Jansen. Loser—Branca. Umpires —Jorda, Conlan, Stewart, Goetz. Time—2:28. Attendance—34,320.

There was no time for celebration. The World Series began the next day at Yankee Stadium. Casey Stengel had Allie Reynolds rested for the opener, but Durocher, with his three regular starters limp from the play-off, had to go with Dave Koslo, who had been a spot starter and occasional reliever during 1951. The Giant magic continued. Koslo scattered seven hits and gave up one run, while Alvin Dark hit a three-run homer and Monte Irvin had four hits and a steal of home. The Giants won, 5–1. Irvin collected three more hits the next afternoon, but none of his mates could do anything with Eddie Lopat, who breezed to a 3–1 win. Larry Jansen pitched well for the Giants, but gave up a homer to Joe Collins in the second inning that helped the Yanks build their lead.

Monte Irvin led the Giants to a 5–1 victory in the opener of the 1951 Series with four hits and a steal of home in the first inning. Bobby Thomson is the surprised Giant batter, and Yogi Berra has the ball an instant too late. The umpire is Bill Summers. *Wide World Photos*

At the Polo Grounds the Giants took a 2–1 game lead by whipping the Yankees, 6–2, in game three. Whitey Lockman's three-run homer capped a five-run Giant outburst in the fifth that chased Vic Raschi and enabled Jim Hearn to gain his first and only World Series victory. The fifth-inning rally started when Eddie Stanky led off the inning with a walk and then reached second on a hit-and-run play that the batter, Al Dark, failed to execute. Stanky was out by six feet at second, but as he slid into Rizzuto's tag, he kicked the ball out of the Yankee shortstop's glove and into center field. Stanky continued to third, scored a moment later, and the rout was on.

More burglary in broad daylight. Eddie Stanky, out by three feet on an attempted steal, has just kicked the ball out of Yankee shortstop Phil Rizzuto's glove. Stanky got up and continued to third. The Giants won the third Series game, 6–1, and took a short-lived lead in games. *Wide World Photos*

For a fleeting moment the Giants looked to be in control of things. A rested Sal Maglie was ready for the fourth game, and Stengel was forced to choose between Reynolds, with two days' rest, or one from a group of lesser men. A downpour came to Casey's rescue. The game was postponed a day and Reynolds was given a precious extra day off. Allie went all the way in the fourth contest and won, 6–2. In the top of the fifth inning Joe DiMaggio belted a two-run homer off Maglie, and even disappointed Giant fans, aware that DiMaggio might be playing in his last Series, cheered as the Yankee Clipper crossed the plate.

In the second game of the Series, Mickey Mantle twisted his knee chasing a fly ball and was sidelined for the duration. This made it possible for another bright Yankee rookie, Gil McDougald, to demonstrate his skills. He had hit .306 in 131 games during 1951, but was overshadowed by Mantle's accomplishments and subsequent publicity. In the third inning of the fifth game McDougald came to bat with the bases loaded and smacked a homer, the first grand-slam hit by a rookie in World Series play. The blast sent Larry Jansen to the showers, but Jansen's successors were no more effective. Run-scoring extra-base hits were hit by DiMaggio, Woodling, and Johnny Mize, and even Phil Rizzuto found the long-ball range with a two-run home run in the fourth. The final score was 13–1, and the Series moved back to Yankee Stadium with the Yanks in need of just one more win.

The Giants hadn't lost two games in a row for weeks, and the fact that the Yankees had administered the successive beatings so effortlessly may have unnerved the National Leaguers. In the sixth game Dave Koslo began shakily,

gave up a run in the first inning, and then three more in the last of the sixth, when Hank Bauer tripled over Monte Irvin's head with the bases loaded. The score was 4–1 in the top of the ninth, at which point the Giants gave every indication that another miracle was forthcoming. They loaded the bases with no outs and had Monte Irvin due at bat, who was then hitting .460. Bob Kuzava relieved Johnny Sain and retired Irvin on a long fly to left that scored a run and moved runners to second and third. The next batter was Bobby Thomson, and the situation was ominously similar to the drama of a week earlier. Thomson connected with Kuzava's second pitch and hit a high fly toward the left-field stands. Giant fans roared as Woodling ran back under the ball, but the cheers died when the ball faded and Woodling caught up to it on the warning track. Another run scored, but with two out the Giants would need a hit to deliver the equalizer. Sal Yvars, pinch-hitting for Hank Thompson, nearly turned the trick. He stroked a low line drive to right that Bauer misjudged for an instant and then had to catch while sliding forward on the seat of his pants. Undignified, perhaps, but it was the third out and meant a third consecutive world championship for the Yankees.

The Yankees went on to defeat the Giants in the 1951 World Series and record their fourteenth world championship. This is the only team DiMaggio and Mantle played together on. Bat boys, left to right: J. Carrieri and J. Cali. Front row, left to right: Yogi Berra, Phil Rizzuto, Billy Martin, Eddie Lopat, coaches Tommy Henrich and Jim Turner, manager Casey Stengel, coaches Frank Crosetti and Bill Dickey, Bobby Hogue, Art Schallock, Gene Woodling, and Charlie Silvera. Second row, left to right: trainer Gus Mauch, Jim Brideweser, Archie Wilson, Jerry Coleman, Bobby Brown, Johnny Hopp, Hank Bauer, Mickey Mantle, Jackie Jensen, Joe Ostrowski, Joe Collins, Vic Raschi. Third row, left to right: Allie Reynolds, Johnny Mize, Gil McDougald, Ernie Nevel, Bob Kuzava, Frank Shea, Johnny Sain, Tom Morgan, Clint Courtney, Ralph Houk, Joe DiMaggio, and Stubby Overmire. *Brown Brothers*

Local players swept all of baseball's prestigious post-season honors. Yogi Berra and Roy Campanella won the Most Valuable Player award in their respective leagues, and Gil McDougald and Willie Mays were named Rookies of the Year. The only gloomy note was Joe DiMaggio's retirement announcement. DiMaggio had the good sense to retire with memories of his magnificence still fresh. He left behind a matchless playing record and a legacy of dignified leadership that no succeeding Yankee player has approached.

In the Yankees' executive office on the day he announced his retirement, Joe DiMaggio posed beneath his own photograph and those of other Yankee superstars and pondered the end of an illustrious career. *N.Y. Daily News Photo*

CHAPTER SEVEN

1952

Four in a Row
for the Old Professor

In 1952 the Korean war draft claimed several essential players from all three teams. The Yankees had already lost Whitey Ford, and early in the season Jerry Coleman and Bobby Brown departed as well. A more critical loss was averted when Mickey Mantle's chronic bone disease, a condition that would plague him throughout his career, classified him 4-F. The Dodgers' threadbare pitching staff was further weakened when Don Newcombe reported for two years of active duty. Newk had won fifty-six games in his first three years in the majors and had established himself as one of the top hurlers in baseball when his number came up. But the Giants suffered the greatest loss. Willie Mays played in only a few games in the spring before the start of his two-year hitch. The Giants would not be the same without him.

The Durochermen suffered an equally devastating setback during an exhibition game with the Indians, when Monte Irvin broke his ankle making an unnecessary slide into third base. It was feared at first that Monte's career was finished, but as treatment progressed, that gloomy prognosis was revised. Irvin would play again, the doctors predicted, but probably not for another year. Monte had played in 151 games during 1951, hit .312, and led the National League with 121 runs batted in. He was thirty by the time he reached the majors, after nearly a decade of play in the Negro Leagues. At age thirty-three, with his leg in a cast from toe to thigh, his future looked bleak.

These reverses notwithstanding, the Giants somehow managed to make a fight of it for the pennant. They captured sixteen of their first eighteen games, and were in first place on Memorial Day. Sal Maglie won nine games in a row during that stretch, and a twenty-eight-year-old rookie named Hoyt Wilhelm came out of the bullpen and hypnotized opposing hitters with his dancing knuckle ball. The Polo Grounders lost some ground in July and August, when Maglie and Larry Jansen suffered back injuries, but they were not finally outdistanced until late September.

Helped by the Giants' misfortunes, the Dodgers managed to win the pennant, but they weren't exactly overpowering. Their team batting average was

Bobby Thomson played third base for the last half of the 1951 season and most of 1952. The manner in which he has captured this pop fly indicates that the hot corner was not a position he was ideally suited to. *UPI Photo*

Andy Pafko, after several outstanding seasons with the Chicago Cubs, joined the Dodgers in 1951 and was their regular left fielder in 1952. A rugged, hustling ballplayer, Pafko could hit with power, was a sure fielder, and had an excellent throwing arm. *N.Y. Daily News Photo*

down thirteen points from 1951; the sluggers Hodges, Snider, and Campanella fell off in home-run and RBI production; and the biggest winner on the mound staff was a rookie reliever named Joe Black, who won only one game in a starting role. But Black made the difference. In fifty-six appearances, he won fifteen games, saved fifteen, and recorded an ERA of 2.15. A routine formula for Dodger success in 1952 was to build a lead late in the game for Joe Black to protect. The Brooks won sixty of their first eighty-two games, slumped late in the season, but had just enough push to carry them to the flag.

A number of uncommon events enlivened the Dodger campaign. In May they beat the Reds, 19–1, scoring fifteen runs in the first inning, during which Peewee Reese managed to reach base three times. On June 19, Carl Erskine pitched a no-hitter against the Cubs that missed being a perfect game when Erskine walked Willard Ramsdell, the Cubs' pitcher, in the third inning. On September 3, the Dodgers had an eight-game lead over the Giants, but ten days later it was cut to three. The Giants were then three games closer to the Dodgers than they had been at that point in 1951. As Brooklyn brooded, the *Saturday Evening Post* published an article titled "Dodgers Won't Blow It Again." The author was Chuck Dressen. With the whammy staring them in the eye, the Dodgers got some help from the Phillies, who beat the Giants three straight times and crushed Polo Grounds hopes for another miracle. Brooklyn clinched the pennant on September 23. For the first time in four years the Dodgers avoided going into the last game of the season before deciding the pennant's outcome.

On June 19, 1952, Carl Erskine pitched a no-hitter over the Chicago Cubs. Only a walk given up to the opposing pitcher, Willard Ramsdell, spoiled an otherwise perfect performance. Peewee Reese, on the left, and Billy Cox made fine fielding plays in support of Erskine. *Wide World Photos*

While the city's National League entries were contesting their championship, the Yankees turned back only moderate resistance in reasserting their superiority in the American League. After floundering around .500 during April and May, they took the lead in June and held it through July. They slumped in August, had a no-hitter thrown at them by Detroit's Virgil "Fire" Trucks, and surrendered first place to the Indians. In mid-September, however, the Yanks beat the Tribe in a critical game at Cleveland and were home free from that point. In that contest they routed hard-throwing Mike Garcia, the Big Bear, who had won twenty games, including his last nine out of ten, and four in a row over the Yankees. He also had a streak of thirty consecutive scoreless innings ended by the Bombers.

Mickey Mantle homered in the 7–1 win over Garcia, slammed twenty-two more during 1952, and finished with a .311 average. Despite his unsteadiness in center field, he more than made up for the statistical loss of Joe DiMaggio. Gene Woodling, Hank Bauer, and Yogi Berra hit well too, especially Yogi, who set an all-time home-run record for American League catchers with thirty.

The Yankee pitching leaders failed to match the sixty-seven wins collected by Cleveland's Early Wynn, Mike Garcia, and Bob Lemon, but Allie Reynolds won twenty games for the first and only time in his career, led the league in strikeouts, and had the majors' best ERA, 2.06. He also appeared as a reliever six times and was credited with six saves. Reynolds' fellow fireballing right-hander, Vic Raschi, failed to win twenty games for the first time in three seasons, but his value to the team was recognized when Stengel named him to start in the All Star game. On July 13, Vic had a no-hitter working against the Tigers until a home run by Joe Ginsberg ruined it with two out in the eighth

Mickey Mantle stands in against Bob Feller of the Cleveland Indians. In his first full season as the Yankee center fielder, Mickey hit .311, belted twenty-three homers, and led American League center fielders with fifteen assists. *UPI Photo*

Above: Billy Loes won thirteen games in 1952 and had an ERA of 2.69. He was signed off the Long Island City sandlots by the Dodgers in 1948, when he was only nineteen, and ended his career in 1961 with the San Francisco Giants. *N.Y. Daily News Photo* *Right:* 1952 Rookie of the Year in the National League, Joe Black, in action against the Yankees in the opener of the 1952 World Series. As a reliever, Black had posted a 15–4 record and a 2.15 ERA. Dressen gambled on him for the first Series game, and Black responded with a 4–2 win. *UPI Photo*

inning. Raschi was ahead in the count, one and two, and could have tempted the Tiger catcher with a bad pitch, but instead he boldly fired the ball into the strike zone, and Ginsberg, a .185 hitter, rapped it into the seats. It was the closest Raschi would ever come to a no-hitter.

In beating the Giants, the Dodgers achieved one of their primary goals in 1952. The other, of course, was to beat the Yankees in the World Series. It was the fourth time in twelve years that the two teams clashed in the October games, and the Brooks were still seeking their first championship.

Reliever or not, the most effective Dodger hurler was Joe Black, and he was Dressen's choice to open the Series against Allie Reynolds at Ebbets Field. Black made Dressen's gamble look like an inspiration. He went all the way, gave up six harmless hits, and the Brooks won, 4–2. It was the first time in their history that the Dodgers had won a Series opener. Duke Snider's two-run homer in the last of the sixth broke a 1–1 tie and evened a score with Reynolds, who had fanned the Duke three times in the first game of the 1949 Series.

A bobble by the usually sure-handed Gil Hodges helped the Yankees rally for five runs in the sixth inning of the second game, and go on to win, 7–1. After Gil dropped what should have been an inning-ending throw, the Bomb-

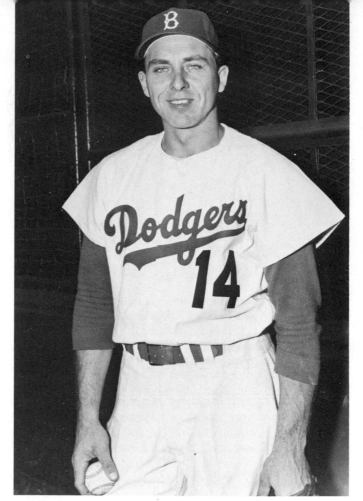

Gil Hodges, the strong man of the Dodgers for fourteen seasons. From 1949 through 1955 he drove in more than a hundred runs each season, and averaged better than thirty-two homers per year. He was a graceful and sure fielder and perhaps the most admired baseball player of his time. *N.Y. Daily News Photo*

ers scored four runs, three on Billy Martin's homer. The total was more than enough for Vic Raschi, who limited the Dodgers to three hits. Carl Erskine, the losing pitcher, injured himself slightly before the game even began. He tumbled off a ladder in the clubhouse, trying to peer out a ceiling-level window to see what the weather was like.

At this point the Series moved to the Bronx, where Yankee Stadium's more forgiving left-field expanse encouraged the employment of left-handed pitchers. Preacher Roe and Eddie Lopat worked eight strong innings each, and in the top of the ninth, with the Dodgers leading, 3–2, Reese and Robinson both scored on a passed ball by Yogi Berra. Johnny Mize hit his first World Series home run in the last of the ninth, but it came with no one on base and still left the Bombers short, 5–3.

Both managers then sent their aces, Black and Reynolds, to the mound with only two days' rest, Dressen in hopes of gaining a decisive edge and Stengel in an effort to even the Series up. Black pitched courageously, but Reynolds won, 2–0, on a homer by Mize and a triple by Mantle, followed by Reese's error that let Mickey score. As a reward for his pinch homer in the third game, Mize was the starting first baseman in the fourth contest. He played nine innings, but admitted after the game, "I can still hit 'em a mile, but I'm getting

Billy Martin, on the left, and Vic Raschi after the Yankees' 7–1 victory in the second
game of the 1952 Series. Raschi pitched a three-hitter, and Martin's three-run homer
in the sixth broke the game open. *N.Y. Daily News Photo*

a little old for this." At the same moment Joe Black sat in front of his locker,
slumped with disappointment, and said, "I'm always failing." Reese overheard
that and sharply reminded Black that it was his relief work that had made it
possible for Brooklyn to be in the World Series in the first place.

The eleven-inning fifth game provided a showcase for Carl Erskine and
Duke Snider. The Dodgers got away to a 4–0 lead, but Erskine squandered
it and gave up five runs in the last of the fifth that included a three-run homer
by the incorrigible Johnny Mize. After Mize's blast, Dressen came to the
mound, and the Stadium crowd watched to see who would emerge from the
Dodger bullpen. No one did. Unaccountably, Dressen decided to leave Erskine
in the game, a decision subject to the most severe second-guessing, but Chuck's
faith was upheld when Erskine retired the next nineteen Yankee batters in a
row. In the meantime Duke Snider drove home the tying run in the seventh,
and then doubled home Billy Cox with the winning tally in the eleventh. It
was the Duke's fourth RBI of the day. The taut drama stretched to the game's
final out. In the bottom of the eleventh Mize connected with an Erskine fast
ball and drove it on a line toward the right-field seats. But Carl Furillo
retreated to the barrier, waited, then leaped and snared the ball one-handed
to save the victory.

The Dodgers needed just one more win in the last two games, both of which
would be played in friendly Ebbets Field. The sixth game witnessed two wasted
home runs by Duke Snider and Billy Loes' losing a ground ball in the sun. Loes
had worked well until the seventh, when a homer by Berra, a single, a balk,

The graceful and powerful swing of Johnny Mize. He hit home runs in the third and fourth Series games, then slammed a three-run homer in the fifth inning of the fifth game. This picture was taken in the last of the eleventh inning after the Dodgers had taken a 6–5 lead, and once again the ball is heading for the right-field stands. *Wide World Photos*

Carl Furillo leaps and makes a game-saving catch of Mize's belt in the last of the eleventh inning of the fifth 1952 World Series game. The Dodgers won the game, 6–5, and took a three-to-two Series edge. *N.Y. Daily News Photo*

and then a single off Billy's knee scored two runs. Mantle's homer in the eighth gave the Bombers a 3–1 lead. In the bottom of the eighth inning Snider hit his second homer of the day, George Shuba doubled, and Stengel replaced Raschi with Reynolds, who got the last four outs. After the game Stengel was asked if he hadn't wanted to save Reynolds for the seventh game. Casey pointed out that if he hadn't used Reynolds in relief, there might not have been a seventh game. "What would I be saving him for then," Casey asked, "the Junior Prom?"

Weary Joe Black started the seventh contest against Ed Lopat, who had been resting since the third game. Each pitched three scoreless innings, then Mr. Mize drove in a run in the top of the fourth inning, which the Dodgers matched in the bottom of the fourth. The teams scored another run apiece in the fifth, but in the sixth Mantle's mighty homer and a sharp single by Mize finally retired Black. The Bombers scored an insurance run in the seventh to lead, 4–2, but suffered some agonizing moments in the last of the seventh before breathing easily. The Dodgers loaded the bases with one out, and Bob Kuzava came on to face Duke Snider. He jammed the Dodger slugger with a curve that was popped into Gil McDougald's glove. The next hitter, Jackie Robinson, worked the count to three and two, and then he too lifted a high pop, but this one seemed to have a tranquilizing effect on the entire Yankee infield. Everyone gazed at the ball admiringly, but made no move to catch it. Billy Martin finally broke out of his trance, dashed madly toward home, and caught the ball on his shoe top. The tying run was halfway home when Billy made his frantic stab. The disheartened Dodgers mounted no threat in the eighth or ninth inning.

In the bottom of the seventh inning of the seventh 1952 Series contest Billy Martin made a running catch of Jackie Robinson's two-out pop-fly hit with the bases loaded. The runner at third has already crossed the plate, and Billy Cox can be seen running toward home with what would have been the tying run had Martin failed to make the catch. *N.Y. Daily News Photo*

It was a brilliant, nerve-shredding World Series, but as far as Brooklyn was concerned it had ended with familiar despondency. The Dodgers had blown a three-to-two game edge in their own ball park and allowed the insatiable Yankees to gain their fourth consecutive world championship.

Overheard as they trudged toward the BMT stairway, a downcast husband and wife exemplified the Brooklyn mood: "You don't gotta give up now, Elsie. Wait 'til next year."

"Wait 'til next year?" Elsie muttered. "They should only choke next year."

Casey Stengel in the clubhouse following the deciding game of the 1952 World Series. He has just captured his fourth successive world championship and is in a playful mood. *Brown Brothers*

CHAPTER EIGHT

1953

Billy the Brat
Buries the Brooks

"Go home, keep the Commandments, and say a prayer for Gil Hodges." Thus did Father Herbert Redmond of St. Francis Xavier Church in Brooklyn conclude 10:00 A.M. Mass on May 17, 1953. The day before, Hodges had been benched for the first time in his career. He had one homer and thirteen singles to show for seventy-five official at bats, and as the Dodgers sagged toward the second division, Manager Dressen felt constrained to take decisive action. Hodges' problems had actually begun late in 1952, but as the Dodgers battled for the pennant, the tall first baseman's slump received scant notice. More noticeable, however, was his 0 for 21 performance in the 1952 World Series, when just an average showing might have made a fundamental difference in the outcome. As Hodges struggled through the first month of the 1953 season, it seemed as if his crisis were affecting the entire team. The Dodgers looked up to the strong, gentle man. It was inevitable that they would suffer with him.

The power of prayer probably had less to do with Hodges' recovery than several hundred feet of movie film taken of his batting form. The film showed Gil moving his lead foot slightly left while striding, thus breaking the rhythm of his swing and leaving him at the mercy of any pitcher adept at hitting the outside corner of the plate. Dressen helped Hodges alter his stance slightly to compensate, and Gil and the Dodgers were soon back in business. Brooklyn won ten games in a row during late May and early June and took over first place.

They held the lead from late June straight through to September 12, which marked the earliest pennant clinching in nearly fifty years. Only the Braves, who had moved from Boston to Milwaukee just before the season opened, provided token resistance. They led the league for a few days in June, before a Brooklyn surge overtook them.

For the first time in years the Dodgers had real depth to their pitching staff. Carl Erskine, Russ Meyer, and Billy Loes formed an effective starting rotation with spot help from Preacher Roe and Johnny Podres. Clem Labine and Jim Hughes took up the slack in the bullpen effort left by the sad decline of Joe

Jim "Junior" Gilliam broke into the Dodger starting lineup in his rookie season, taking over at second base and moving Jackie Robinson to left field. Monte Irvin of the Giants is safe at second in this picture, but Gilliam's throw to first was in time to nip Wes Westrum. The umpire is Augie Donatelli. *UPI Photo*

Black. Jackie Robinson, despite moving to left field to make room for Jim "Junior" Gilliam at second, hit .329 and drove in ninety-five runs. And Chuck Dressen had another go at predicting, although his "The Giants is dead" pronouncement was on considerably safer ground than the one made in the *Saturday Evening Post* a year earlier. When Dressen made his remark about the Giants on August 11, the Polo Grounders were in fifth place, sixteen and a half games behind the front-running Brooks.

The Yankees lost on opening day, but from that point on played as if determined to clinch the pennant by Father's Day. In early June they won eighteen games in a row, and by the middle of the month led Cleveland by ten and a half games. A nine-game losing streak followed, but no one could take advantage of it. The White Sox did move to within five games during the first week of August, but over the weekend of August 7 they were welcomed rudely to Yankee Stadium by Eddie Lopat, Whitey Ford, and Bob Kuzava, who allowed one run in twenty-seven innings and discouraged further pursuit.

Kuzava was a good example of the mythical "pin-stripe effect." There was a theory that the simple act of donning a Yankee uniform could sharpen the skills of the mediocre and revitalize the aging. Other examples included Johnny Mize, Ewell Blackwell, Johnny Hopp, Irv Noren, and Johnny Sain, and a few years later Don Larsen, Dale Long, and Bobby Shantz. Essential contributions were made by these players, who, for one reason or another, had been discarded by previous employers.

Another Yankee legend was born in 1953: the tape-measure home run. On April 17, Mickey Mantle teed off on the Senators' Chuck Stobbs and drove a homer over Griffith Stadium's center-field wall. The wall was 55 feet high and 460 feet from home plate, and someone calculated that the ball traveled 565 feet before touching down. It was also pointed out that it might have gone

Above: Second baseman Davey Williams on the left, with catcher Wes Westrum. Each was a defensive standout, Westrum made just one error in 139 games during the 1950 season, and they both hit a grand-slam home run in the same game against the Cardinals in 1951, to tie a major-league record. *N.Y. Daily News Photo*   *Below:* Steady and dependable Joe Collins, on the left, played with the Yankees for ten years and appeared in seven World Series. Next to Collins is Gil McDougald, who appeared in World Series contests eight out of the ten years he played for the Yankees. McDougald is seventh on the list of World Series home-run hitters. *N.Y. Daily News Photo*

farther had it not grazed the side of the scoreboard. From then on it was no longer enough to just hit a home run. The feat had to be validated by a publicist armed with a tape measure and comparative statistics.

Giant publicists, on the other hand, were hard pressed to sugarcoat the effects of Leo Durocher's temper tantrums and public sulking. After a series of screaming arguments with various umpires in June, Leo was summoned to National League president Warren Giles' office. Leo apologized to the umpires

Above: **The captains. Alvin Dark, on the left, had three successive .300 seasons beginning in 1951, and banged out a career high of twenty-three home runs in 1953. Peewee Reese played with the Dodgers for sixteen seasons. In the seventh game of the 1955 World Series he threw out Elston Howard in the ninth to retire the Yankees and give Brooklyn its first world championship.** *N.Y. Daily News Photo*
Below: **His hand still bandaged from his fight with Leo Durocher, Carl Furillo points to the distance marker on the Yankee Stadium right-field barrier. It was the same figure with which Furillo won the National League batting title. Despite his injury, Furillo was in the lineup the next day for the opener of the 1953 World Series.** *N.Y. Daily News Photo*

There were no soft spots in the 1953 Dodger lineup. These six—left to right: Carl Furillo, Duke Snider, Roy Campanella, Billy Cox, Jackie Robinson, and Gil Hodges—combined for a composite batting average of .319. They also contributed 157 home runs and 621 runs batted in. *N.Y. Daily News Photo*

the next day, and added, "In all my years in baseball, I've never questioned the integrity of the umpires." In September, during a series with the Dodgers, Leo got into a wrestling match with Carl Furillo after Furillo was hit by Ruben Gomez and taunted by the Giant manager from the safety of the New York dugout. Furillo touched first, called time, and strode to the Giant bench. He was met at the top of the dugout stairs by Durocher, forty-eight years old, bald, but game, and the two swung at each other, tumbled to the ground, and thrashed about like schoolboys. They were soon parted, but not before someone planted a spiked shoe on Furillo's left hand and fractured a bone. Furillo was sidelined for the rest of the season, but his .344 average proved unbeatable by the rest of the league's hitters.

With Maglie and Jansen still ailing, it became clear early in the season that the Giants weren't going anywhere. Monte Irvin and Bobby Thomson had good years, but the biggest winner on the mound staff was rookie Ruben Gomez with just thirteen victories. Maglie and Jansen combined for nineteen wins, twenty-seven fewer than they produced in 1951. The Giants finished fifth, thirty-five games behind the Dodgers, and anxiously awaited the return of Willie Mays.

The Dodgers spent the last two weeks of the season itching to get at the Yankees. They posted a 46–11 record from the All Star game through Labor Day, and finished with 105 wins and 49 losses, a club record. They had the league's leading hitter in Furillo, their eight starting regulars combined for a group average of .308, and Snider, Hodges, and Campanella powered 114

In contrast to the Dodger might shown in the preceding photo, the Yankees had only two .300 hitters, Gene Woodling, on the left, and Hank Bauer. But each was a superb defensive outfielder and a dangerous clutch hitter. Through three World Series, starting in 1956, Bauer hit safely in seventeen straight games. *Wide World Photos*

homers and 390 runs batted in. The entire Yankee team could only produce 113 homers. Roy Campanella was later named the National League's Most Valuable Player, but the most heartening accomplishment belonged to Gil Hodges, who recovered from his spring miseries to hit .302, belt thirty-one homers, and drive in 122 runs. Carl Erskine won twenty games, and Dodger hurlers led the majors in strikeouts. Surely this was the year the Yankees could be taken.

It was the fiftieth World Series, and it began disastrously for Brooklyn. In the opening game at Yankee Stadium, Carl Erskine started and was quickly replaced when the Yankees took a first-inning 4–0 lead. Home runs by Gilliam, Hodges, and Shuba tied the score, 5–5, at the end of six and a half, but Joe Collins homered for the Yanks in the last of the seventh, and capped a three-run burst in the eighth with a run-scoring single. The Bombers won, 9–5. The second game matched the teams' venerable southpaws, Lopat and Roe. The Preacher worked six strong innings, but was undone by a Billy Martin homer in the seventh and Mickey Mantle's two-run shot in the last of the eighth. Lopat gave up nine hits but only two runs, while his mates were scoring four.

"EGAD, MEN—WAKE UP!" urged the Brooklyn *Eagle*'s headline on the day of the third game. The scene shifted to Brooklyn, but the scenario didn't change. The Yankees took a 1–0 lead in the top of the fifth inning, Vic Raschi had given the Dodgers nothing in four frames, and Ebbets Field was cloaked with gloom. But in the bottom of the fifth Billy Cox squeezed home the tying run, and in the last of the sixth Jackie Robinson's run-scoring single gave the Brooks a 2–1 lead and rekindled hopes for a decent Dodger showing. Two innings later the Yankees tied the score, but in the bottom of the eighth Roy Campanella gave the Dodgers the lead again.

Meanwhile, Carl Erskine, given another chance after his brief appearance in the first game, was threatening a World Series record for strikeouts in a single game. He had fanned Mantle and Collins four times each, and going into the top of the ninth had struck out a total of twelve, one short of the mark set in 1929. The first Yankee batter was a left-handed pinch hitter named Don Bollweg, who went down on three quick swings. The record was equaled, but out came another pinch hitter, Johnny Mize, a considerably more intimidating figure. Mize loved to hit against the Dodgers, but Erskine barely gave Jawn a chance to get the bat off his shoulder. Carl tied him up with two curve balls and then blazed a fast ball down and in. Mize swung and missed, Erskine had his record, and one out later the Dodgers had their first victory.

A day later, on the strength of timely extra-base hits and Billy Loes' pitching, the Dodgers evened the Series with a 7–3 win. Before the game Loes told a reporter that an Ebbets Field assignment was "like pitchin' in a phone booth," but it turned out that Loes' adversary, Whitey Ford, was more afflicted with claustrophobia. It was Whitey's first Ebbets Field start, and he went the way of most southpaws unwise in the ways of the Brooklyn bandbox: to the showers. The last out of the game was particularly satisfying to the Dodgers.

Roy Campanella and Carl Erskine, after Erskine struck out fourteen Yankees in the third game of the Series to set an all-time record. Campy's homer in the last of the eighth inning won the game for the Dodgers, 3–2. *N.Y. Daily News Photo*

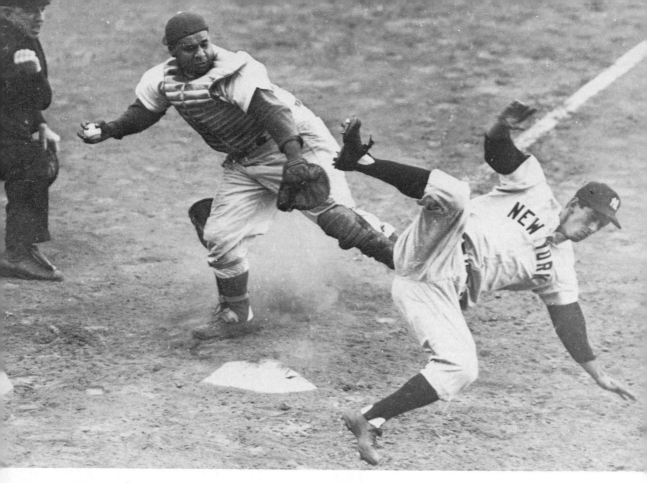

Billy Martin, sent flying by the force of his collision at home plate with husky Roy Campanella. Martin tried to score from second on Mantle's single to left, and was cut down for the final out. The Dodgers won the game, 7–3, and tied the Series at two games apiece. *N.Y. Daily News Photo*

Billy Martin had been stinging the Brooks with base hits and slick fielding through the first four games, but with two out in the ninth he tried to score from second on a sharply hit single and was thrown out at the plate. He ran into Roy Campanella at the plate in an effort to jar the ball loose, but the collision sent the slender Yankee second baseman spinning through the air like a rag doll.

The pivotal fifth game produced eighteen runs and twenty-five hits, much to the discomfort of seven embattled hurlers. Brooklyn outhit the Yanks, but finished on the short end of an 11–7 score. The big blow came in the top of the third, with the score tied, 1–1, and the bases full of Yankees. Russ Meyer relieved Johnny Podres, and Mickey Mantle deposited his first pitch in the upper level of the center-field grandstand. Billy Martin and Gil McDougald homered later in the game, as did Billy Cox and Jim Gilliam, but the Dodgers

In a slugfest, the Yankees won the fifth game of the 1953 Series, 11–7. This picture shows Yankee shortstop Phil Rizzuto skidding into third just in time to beat the throw to substitute third baseman Bobby Morgan. *N.Y. Daily News Photo*

were not able to overcome a 10–2 Yankee lead. The beneficiary of that advantage was Jim McDonald, who needed help in the eighth but got credit for the victory. Yankee firepower had provided a vital extra day of rest for Whitey Ford.

The Series then moved back to Yankee Stadium, and Chuck Dressen had no choice but to start Carl Erskine, with two days' rest, in an effort to stave off the Yankee clincher. Carl was not quite equal to the task. The Bombers scored twice in the first and again in the second, and Whitey Ford worked smoothly through seven innings, giving up just one run. In the top of the ninth Ford weakened and was replaced by Allie Reynolds, who walked Duke Snider and then gave up a home run to Carl Furillo that tied the score at three apiece. A dramatic shot, to be sure, but it only succeeded in giving Billy Martin a chance to end the Series with a flourish. In the last of the ninth, with one out and runners on first and second, Martin capped his brilliant Series performance with a bouncing single through the middle that scored the winning run and gave the Yankees their unprecedented and unequaled fifth world championship in a row.

Hank Bauer stomps on home plate with the run that won the sixth game and gave the Yankees their fifth successive world championship. Bauer scored on Billy Martin's last-of-the-ninth-inning single. It was Martin's twelfth hit of the Series. Frankie Crosetti follows Bauer home, Gil McDougald waits to welcome the Yankee runner, and Campy, observing a painfully familiar ritual, walks off in defeat. *N.Y. Daily News Photo*

After the Series, Johnny Mize retired, with a fifteen-year lifetime average of .312. Shortly after that it was announced that Chuck Dressen would not be returning as Dodger manager. Dressen and Dodger president Walter O'Malley had quarreled, Dressen had quit, and a week later Chuck's wife wrote O'Malley a letter scolding the owner for his policy of signing managers to one-year contracts. Dressen wondered out loud how a fifth-place manager (Durocher) rated a two-year contract, as had other also-rans. O'Malley expressed regrets over Dressen's departure, but did not change his policy. Later that fall Dressen signed to manage the Oakland Oaks of the Pacific Coast League.

In December, O'Malley announced that the Dodgers were considering three building sites in Brooklyn for the construction of a new ball park. The Dodger president promised that "within five years, the Dodgers will definitely have a new stadium." He kept that promise.

CHAPTER NINE

The Ball Parks

Each of the city's ball parks had its own distinct identity, an identity remarkably well suited to the team it housed. The stately magnificence of Yankee Stadium was appropriately the home of the haughty and successful Yankees. The Polo Grounds, like the Giants, was a venerable institution, cherishing the memory of a time when the two were synonymous with New York baseball. And the cozy, riotous atmosphere of Ebbets Field provided the Dodgers with a zany image that even their dignified championship teams could not completely dispel.

In 1920 the Yankees were informed by the Giants that they were no longer welcome at the Polo Grounds and would have to find their own quarters. Thanks to the prodigious home-run exploits of Babe Ruth, the Yankees' attendance had surpassed the Giants', a circumstance the landlords found embarrassing. Yankee owner Jacob Ruppert bought up some land in the Bronx, negotiated a final two-year lease for his home games at the Polo Grounds, and began construction of a new stadium. It was ready in time for the opening of the 1923 season, a soaring, spectacular arena, with three grandstand tiers, the largest seating capacity in the major leagues, and a fabulous price tag to go with it all. At least, $2,500,000 seemed fabulous at the time. The May 1923 issue of *Baseball Magazine* described the new ball park shortly before the start of the season.

THE YANKEES' NEW HOME, BASEBALL'S LARGEST AND COSTLIEST STADIUM

By F. C. Lane

Travellers approaching New York from the sea are greeted by the lofty torch of the Statue of Liberty. Visitors arriving from the north over the tracks of the New York Central or the New Haven Railroads are confronted by the imposing pile of the new Yankee Stadium. The approaches to the world's metropolis are appropriate in either case. To the sojourner from Europe, New York means opportunity. To the visitor from other parts of America, New York is the amusement center of the continent. And that spirit of diversion finds fitting expression in this colossal monument of athletic sport.

The Yankee Stadium is indeed the last word in ball parks. But not the least of its merits is its advantage of position. From the plain of the Harlem River it looms up like the great Pyramid of Cheops from the sands of Egypt.

The historic Polo Grounds just across the muddy Harlem nestles in a cove at

The big ball park. For more than half a century it has been the most famous stadium in the world. This is how Yankee Stadium looked in the 1950s, rooted in the bustling Bronx, its ornate frieze decorating the edge of the roof. *N.Y. Daily News Photo*

the foot of Coogan's Bluff and the broad sweep of its curving grandstand is lost against the craggy background of cliffs bristling with apartment houses. The Yankee Stadium suffers from no such contrast. It fairly dominates the whole Harlem River Valley. There is nothing behind it but blue sky. Stores and dwellings and the rolling hills of the Bronx are too far removed to interfere with this perspective. The Polo Grounds are lost in the infinite detail of Manhattan Island. The Yankee Stadium stands out in bold relief and the measuring eye gives it full credit for every ounce of cement and every foot of structural steel that went into its huge frame. As an anonymous spectator remarked viewing the new park from the bridge which spans the Harlem, "Big as it is, it looks even bigger."

. . .

Nearly ten acres of valuable city real estate are embraced within the outer wall of the Yankee Stadium. Of this large tract some four acres is appropriated by the diamond and playing field. The recently constructed diamond is of the approved turtle-backed type. The distance from home plate to the stands along the right and left field foul lines is approximately equal to the distance between home plate and the right field wall at the Polo Grounds. It will therefore be just as easy to hit a home run into the right field stands in the Yankee Stadium and a shade easier into the left field stands close to the foul line. From the foul lines, however, the stands recede rapidly into the distance and it would take a terrific wallop even from Babe Ruth's huge bat to drive a ball into the remoter section of the bleachers.

Foolish stories have floated about that the playing field was designedly limited so as to enable Babe Ruth to break his home run record. One needs but to glance at these stories to see their falsity. Babe Ruth is at the best a temporary attraction. A few seasons at the most and his great feats will be but a memory. The Yankee Stadium, however, is a permanent institution. It was built not as a setting for one player, however brilliant a star. It was built to accommodate the teeming thousands of baseball spectators in the world's greatest city.*

Mr. Lane's convictions notwithstanding, the inviting right-field grandstand was constructed with the Bambino very much in mind. Then, as now, home-run hitters were box office, and Babe Ruth was the hottest property in baseball. On opening day his three-run blast off Howard Ehmke of the Red Sox helped the Yankees to a 4–1 victory before a somewhat swollen estimate of 74,000 spectators. Ruth hit forty more homers that season while leading his team to the pennant and a World Series victory over the Giants. The Babe did not, however, clout the first World Series homer in the new stadium. That honor fell to a bandy-legged outfielder for the Giants named Casey Stengel. The two

*© 1923 by Guild Press, Ltd. Reprinted by permission.

A panoramic view of spacious, sweeping Yankee Stadium, filled to capacity for the third game of the 1950 World Series. It was the first triple-tiered stadium and had an official seating capacity of 67,000. It was named "The Home of Champions." *Brown Brothers*

Yankee Stadium's bleachers were more than 500 feet from home plate, but they were always filled for a World Series game. This photo was taken halfway through the third game of the 1950 Series, and the scoreboard shows the lineups and the Yankees leading, 1–0. *Brown Brothers*

Giant victories in the 1923 Series came on homers by the man who thirty years later would lead the Yankees to some of their greatest seasons.

The Stadium and its immediate neighborhood are undergoing extensive renovation. The big ball park will not look the same, but at least it wasn't abandoned. The decision to stay in the Bronx, rather than move to the New Jersey swamps, may indicate a healthier trend in stadium planning.

For several seasons prior to the turn of the century, the New York Giants shared newspaperman James Gordon Bennett's polo field in upper Manhattan for their home games. When this arrangement no longer proved mutually convenient, the Giants moved farther uptown, leased some land from the Harriet Coogan family, and in 1891 built the original Polo Grounds. The park was leveled by fire in 1911, but rebuilt a few months later, and then enlarged in 1923, the same year Yankee Stadium opened. At that point it had acquired its distinctive horseshoe shape, with the covered, double-deck grandstand extending around to the open bleachers and clubhouse in deepest center field. In its over seventy years of existence the park was a stage for most of baseball's greatest stars: Mathewson, McGraw, Ruth, Hubbell, Frisch, Terry, Ott, and Mays, as well as visiting future Hall of Famers. In 1964 it finally gave way to the inexorable sprawl of apartment houses, after witnessing, no doubt with some aristocratic dismay, the antics of the infant New York Mets.

The Harlem River and a ten-cent subway ride were all that separated Yankee Stadium and the Polo Grounds in 1951. This picture was taken during the first World Series game in 1951. Yankee Stadium is jammed, while the Polo Grounds stands empty and quiet. Two days later the action moved across the river. *N.Y. Daily News Photo*

Thirteen-year-old Jerry Schwab, by virtue of living beneath the left-field grandstand of the Polo Grounds, fulfilled the happiest fantasies of thousands of teen-age boys. In 1950, Giant president Horace Stoneham, dissatisfied with the condition of his playing field, approached Matty Schwab, the head grounds keeper at Ebbets Field, with an offer to join the Giants. Matty was hesitant, since he didn't want to commute from Brooklyn, nor was he anxious to take on the house-hunting hassle. Stoneham came up with a perfect solution. He built a two-bedroom apartment right underneath the left-field grandstand and offered it to the Schwab family rent free. For Jerry Schwab it was a paradise. He was allowed to work out occasionally with the players, and when the team was on the road or not scheduled to play, he and his friends had exclusive access to a four-acre playground. And on a warm summer night it was a perfect place to camp out. Imagine what it must have been like, stretched out on the grass, sheltered by the huge curve of the dark grandstand, listening for the hollow shout of a ghostly spectator somewhere in the seats or the spike crunch of a phantom ballplayer on the field.

In an interview for *Collier's* in 1956, Rose Schwab said she liked the apartment very much, even though it did get noisy at times. Matty Schwab added, "It would be hard to take if the Giants ever move to another park. Even if I found a place to live across the street, I'd still feel like a commuter." A year later the Giants broke Matty Schwab's heart, along with those of several hundred thousand past and present Giant fans. One of them was Roger Angell, and in the May 1958 issue of *Holiday,* in an article titled "Farewell, My

Unfortunately, the Polo Grounds was not always filled to the extent seen here during a crucial doubleheader with the Dodgers in 1952. Above the grandstand Coogan's Bluff is visible, shouldering the weight of apartment buildings. *UPI Photo*

A view of the Polo Grounds, with its abbreviated foul lines and yawning center-field expanse. This picture was taken during the fifth game of the 1951 World Series, and shows Gil McDougald hitting a grand-slam home run off the Giants' Sal Maglie. *Wide World Photos*

After the last New York Giants home game a square section of sod was cut out of center field and flown to San Francisco. Manager Bill Rigney participated in the strange ceremony. The grounds keeper squatting down on the left is Matty Schwab, who lived with his family in an apartment under the left-field grandstand. *Wide World Photos*

Giants!," he recorded some of his Polo Grounds memories, including the last game played there by the New York Giants.

Like the team itself, the Polo Grounds is an absurd and lovely thing. It is the only ball park built against a cliff—Coogan's Bluff—so that a patron could walk downhill to his seat. (I loved this approach before a night game. You came slowly down the John T. Brush stairs in the cool of the evening, looking down at the flags and at the tiers of brilliant floodlights on the stands and, beyond them, at the softer shimmer of lights on the Harlem River. Sometimes there was even a moon, rising right out of the Bronx. As you came closer and were fingering for your ticket in your pocket, you could hear brave music from the loudspeakers, broken by the crack of a fungo bat, and through a space in the upper deck you caught a glimpse of grass, soft and incredibly green, in the outfield. You walked faster, tasting excitement in your mouth and with it—every single time—the conviction of victory.)

The Polo Grounds had a crazy name and crazy dimensions. Nobody ever played polo there; the name moved uptown with the team in 1891. In shape, it was closer to a bowling alley than a ball field. Along the foul lines, the right field and left field stands were only 258 and 280 feet from home plate. As a result, hundreds of games were won and lost on measly pop-fly "homers" that would have been caught on a grammar-school field. But the stands receded sharply and almost endlessly toward the center-field bleachers, a fearsome 425 to 450 feet away. Straightaway sluggers loathed the field, because a really noble smash to center, good for a homer in any other park, only amounted to a loud and discouraging out. In modern times, only Joe Adcock of the Braves ever managed to hit a ball into those bleachers on the fly. The clubhouse was behind center field, so that a pitcher knocked out of a game had to walk a long, long way before he could hide his shame.

The history of the Polo Grounds is full and lively—and not exclusively connected with the Giants. The stands burned down in 1911, and the team played part of that season at the field of the New York Highlanders (later the Yankees) at Broadway and 168th Street. From 1913 to 1923, the Yankees were tenants at the Polo Grounds, and it was here that Babe Ruth started hitting the homers that were eventually to pay for Yankee Stadium. Here, too, Dempsey knocked out Firpo. Here Red Grange made his professional debut, playing for the Chicago Bears against the football Giants. And here, one Sunday a few years ago, a fan was shot dead in his seat by a .22 bullet fired from a nearby rooftop. But for most New Yorkers, the Polo Grounds will really be remembered as a lovely place in which to watch the Giants play. The seats were uncomfortable, but the stands were close to the field, and it was nice up there on a sunny June afternoon, watching the action below and seeing, away out in center field, the little shed roofs over the bull-pen benches, where the relief pitchers sat with their legs crossed and their hats tipped over their eyes.

. . . .

I went to the last New York Giants game of them all in the Polo Grounds— September 29, 1957—taking my nine-year-old daughter with me. It was her first major-league game. It was a fine, cool day, the flags were flying, and we sat in the upper deck. There were some dull, touching ceremonies before the game, when a lot of the old-timers who had turned up to say good-by were introduced. George Burns was there and Larry Doyle and Rube Marquard and Carl Hubbell. Bill Rigney presented a bouquet of roses to Mrs. McGraw, and Bobby Thomson pointed to the left-field seats for the photographers. "When is it going to start?" my daughter asked.

It finally did start, but it wasn't much of a game. Willie made a fine catch and throw in the first inning, but that was about all there was. The Pirates ran up the score, and the Giants looked terrible. The stands were half-empty and the crowd was the quietest I have ever heard at any game. Between each inning, a mournful-looking gentleman in the next section to us stood up and displayed a hand-lettered sign that said, "Giant Fan 55 Years." In the eighth inning, I heard a spectator behind me murmur, "Well, at least the Dodgers lost too." The Pirates won, 9–1.

There was a little excitement right after the game when some history-minded fans dug up home-plate and several chunks of outfield turf for souvenirs. A small crowd gathered outside the clubhouse steps to shout their farewells, but we didn't join them. On our way out of the park, my daughter looked at me rather anxiously and said, "I had a good time. That was fun. I'm sorry they lost."

I didn't feel anything—nothing at all. I guess I just couldn't believe it. But it's true, all right. The flags are down, the lights in the temple are out, and the Harlem River flows lonely to the sea.*

Pigtown was a section of Brooklyn located midway between the Bedford section and Flatbush. In the early 1900s it was a slum, but Charles Hercules Ebbets chose it as the location for his new ball park, convinced that a "suburban" location would be more viable than his outmoded and overcrowded facility at Fourth Avenue and Third Street. Thus Ebbets Field was born, named after the colorful president of the Brooklyn baseball club. He died in 1925, the day before the Giants were scheduled to open a series in Brooklyn.

A photo of Ebbets Field, taken shortly after the Second World War. The atmosphere in and around the park was unique and made a visit there a treat unequaled in any ball park before or since. *Brown Brothers*

It was suggested that the opening game be postponed, but manager "Uncle Wilbert" Robinson prevailed against that notion, contending that "Charley wouldn't want anyone to miss a Giant-Brooklyn game just because he died."

Ebbets Field took several years to complete, and there was much eager anticipation of its official opening. The following article appeared in the April 20, 1912, issue of *Sporting Life,* a then popular weekly newspaper that proclaimed itself "devoted to baseball and trapshooting."

EBBETS FIELD WILL HAVE EVERY COMFORT FOR BROOKLYN PATRONS. PRESIDENT EBBETS WILL LEAVE NO STONE UNTURNED, AND NEGLECT NO DETAIL IN THE EMBELLISHMENT OF HIS MAGNIFICENT NEW BALL PARK

BROOKLYN, N.Y. MARCH 15. Charles Ebbets, president of the Brooklyn club, and builder of Magnificent Inspiration, will do nothing by halves in building the new home for his team in the Flatbush section of Brooklyn. In his latest announcement about the park he says, "Public telephone booths will be distributed at various points in the stands; desks will be provided for the accommodation of business men and physicians who may expect sudden telephone calls, to whom messages will be delivered immediately. A room will be provided where articles may be checked free, lost articles reclaimed upon proper identification and umbrellas loaned for a small fee. Another innovation never before used in baseball parks will be the installation of a device whereby announcements of batteries, changes in lineup, and other such information as may be necessary will be furnished to the patrons simultaneously in clear tones, and thus avoid the annoying feature of indistinct announcements very often made under the present method. In the preparation of the plans the aim has been to provide for the comfort, convenience, and safety of the baseball public, and when completed Ebbets Field will be about the most modern, comfortable, perfectly appointed, and conveniently located baseball park in the world.

There were, of course, several significant exceptions to this glowing account. The park did not actually open for another twelve months, and when it did, one of the details neglected was a press box. And the device referred to concerning a modern means for conveying information about the game turned out to be an electric scoreboard, an innovation that did not actually appear for quite a few more seasons.

The compact dimensions of Ebbets Field were determined by the location of streets and plot boundaries, and the right-field playing area abutted Bedford Avenue, with only a twenty-foot wall topped by a twenty-foot screen separating the ballplayers from the adjacent neighborhood. It was this wall and screen that challenged the superb skills of Carl Furillo. In an article for *Collier's* in 1954, Tom Meany wrote that the wall had as many angles as a full-scale Senate investigation. Furillo could describe at least fourteen angles that a ball could come off at, caused by the uneven bounce-back of the mesh screen, the slope of the foam-rubber-padded bottom portion of the wall, and the sharp corner formed by the junction of the wall and scoreboard. Furillo became a virtuoso at fielding balls hit against the wall and screen, and this facility, coupled with a sure and powerful throwing arm, enabled him to lead the league in outfield assists in 1950 and 1951. At that point a Brooklyn writer's warning, "Proceed carefully, the man is armed," was taken to heart. It is also worth noting that

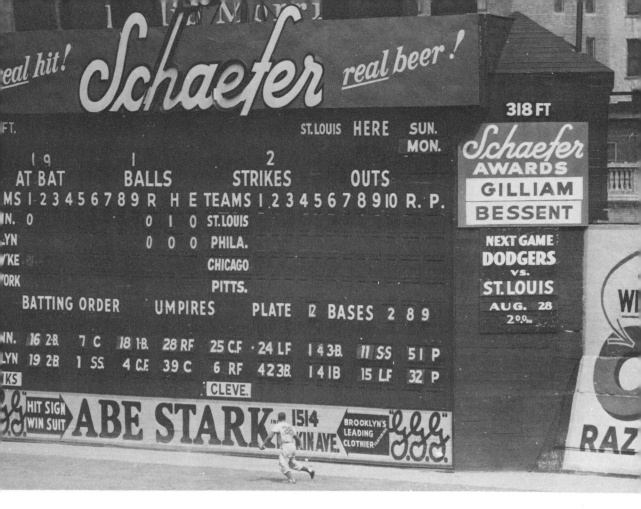

The Ebbets Field scoreboard added an extra measure of difficulty to the eccentric contours of the ball park's right field wall. Here Reds-outfielder Wally Post is seen chasing down Jim Gilliam's double in an August 1956 game. *N.Y. Daily News Photo*

For nearly forty years the Dodger clubhouse custodian was three-hundred-pound "Senator" John Griffin, whose pride in keeping the Dodger house in order is evident in this picture. This photo was taken late in 1956. A year later the clubhouse would remain empty and silent. *Wide World Photos*

while Furillo was on duty, no enemy batter collected a suit offered by a Brooklyn clothier in return for hitting his advertisement on the base of the scoreboard.

The other side of the Bedford Avenue barrier had a unique vitality, as recorded in a *New Yorker* article of October 3, 1953.

OUTSIDE

You know how, when somebody hits a home run in right field at Ebbets Field, Red Barber describes the ball as clearing the fence and descending upon Bedford Avenue? Well, with the Series descending upon us, we got to wondering what happens to all those out-of-the-park balls, so we went right over to Bedford Avenue and found out. The first thing we learned was that shagging home-run baseballs is big business in that neighborhood. Whenever the Dodgers are playing at home, a sizable army of children assembles just beyond the fence, waiting and hoping. They want the Dodgers to win, of course, but what they want most is home runs, no matter who hits them. If dated and autographed by the player who hit it, a ball that was worth three dollars brand-new can be peddled as a souvenir for upward of five dollars. That's the summer price; during the Series the price naturally goes much higher. The best customers for souvenir baseballs are fathers eager to take something home to Junior. The player most likely to provide something for Junior is Duke Snider. A month or so ago, the Duke hit a home run over the right-centerfield scoreboard that wrecked a window at Young Motors, a Plymouth–De Soto salesroom on the far side of Bedford Avenue. The Duke may have been taking it sort of easy that day. Ten or twelve times a summer, when he really puts his back into it, he knocks letters off the Young Motors sign, several feet above the show window. Everybody at Young Motors roots for the Duke, though. Glad to have the sign and window go in a good cause.

Most of the private houses and apartment buildings on Bedford Avenue are far enough away from the field to be out of danger, but a service station—named, perhaps inevitably, the Dodger's Service Station—occupies an even more vulnerable spot than Young Motors. It's at the corner of Bedford and Sullivan Place, beyond the right-field fence, and nearly any first-class left-hand wallop is apt to end up hopping among the pumps. (Because the grandstand at Ebbets Field serves as a shield for the left-field corner, most of the balls that land outside the park are hit by left-handers.) We talked to one of the station attendants, and he told us that a couple of years back, and as sure as he was standing there, a home-run ball went through the roof of a convertible he was servicing, out the side window of the convertible, then rolled through the open door of the station and ended up against the belly of a cat who was asleep there and didn't even bother to wake up—just curled her paws around the ball and went on snoozing. He estimates the distance from home plate to the station at four hundred feet; the height of the Ebbets Field wall and fence is forty feet. Many of the Dodger players stop at the station for gas and repairs, and some of them leave their cars there during games. As the attendant was telling us these things, who should arrive in a powder-blue Cadillac but Preacher Roe, with Carl Erskine on the seat beside him. "Hi ya, Preach!" the attendant cried. Preach said to fill her up.

After every Dodger game, several hundred adults and children gather at the station for a few minutes of happy communion with their heroes. One of these heroes is Gil Hodges, who, the attendant said regretfully, is right-handed and doesn't hit into Bedford Avenue except when he fouls. Another right-handed

hero who has never quite found the range is Roy Campanella. Brightening, the attendant went on to say that he could always tell by the sound of the bat when a ball was coming over the fence; it gives off a hard, sharp ring, just like a cash register. "I used to shag balls myself," he said. "Then I get a couple of pairs of glasses busted and a sprained wrist and I say to myself, 'Listen, you're getting too old for this stuff. Let the balls come to you, not you to the balls.'" At that, he's been luckier than some people. Earlier this season, an impatient motorist stopped at the station, got out of his car, opened the hood, and started checking the water in his battery. A moment later, a homer sailed over the fence and landed on top of the hood, which closed over the motorist's head with a thud. The motorist survived, tried to threaten the Dodgers out of a hundred dollars, and settled for sixty-five. "Didn't deserve a dime," said the attendant. "It should have been me, not him, checking that battery."*

On July 25, 1949, Stan Musial hit for the cycle in leading his team to a 14–1 defeat of the Dodgers. The Cardinal slugger loved to hit in Ebbets Field and enjoyed numerous productive afternoons and evenings there. *N.Y. Daily News Photo*

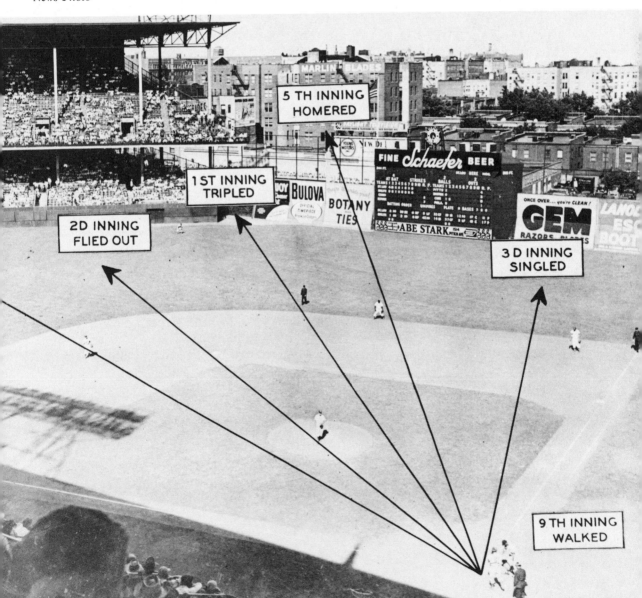

Bedford Avenue, where the Duke used to hit them and where long lines of the Faithful would wait for bleacher seats and sometimes standing-room tickets. This picture was taken early in the morning on the day of the first 1952 World Series game. *UPI Photo*

Ebbets Field had too few rest rooms, overcrowded concessions, inadequate parking, and, from a businessman's point of view, a profit-limiting seating capacity. And it was, in the final analysis, a business consideration that transferred the Dodgers to Los Angeles and sentenced the rickety old park at the corner of Bedford and Sullivan to demolition. Walter O'Malley flirted capriciously with New York City legislators and promoters for over a year, but in October 1957 the final decision to move was made. Since the season had ended by then, the last Brooklyn Dodger game was mercifully spared pathetic farewells such as those witnessed at the Polo Grounds. No fervent speeches or sonorous roll calls of past heroes could have adequately conveyed the spirit or recalled the magic of Ebbets Field. In an affectionate parody of Joyce Kilmer's "The House with Nobody in It," *Herald Tribune* sports editor Bob Cooke wrote an obituary.

THE PARK WITH NOBODY IN IT

By Bob Cooke

Whenever I go to Flatbush, on the subway BMT
I pass by a poor old ball park, where the turnstiles rust by degree.
I know I've passed it a hundred times but I always stop for a minute.
And look at the park, the tragic park, the park with nobody in it.

And this park on the road to Flatbush needs thirty thousand pairs of eyes
And somebody ought to cheer it up, by coming out there under the skies
It needs new life and laughter and the seats should be occupied
'Cause what it needs the most of all are some people sitting inside.

Now if I had a lot of money and all my debts were paid
I'd put a gang of men to work with brush and saw and spade
I'd buy that park and fill it up the way it used to be
With fellows like Snider and Hodges and a great guy named Pee Wee.

They say the park isn't haunted, but I hear there are such things
That hold the talk of Dodgers, their mirth and sorrowings,
I know this park isn't haunted but I wish it were I do
'Cause it wouldn't be so lonely if it had a ghost or two.

A park that has done what a park should do, a park that has sheltered life
That has put its loving concrete arms around a Dodger fan and his wife
A park that has echoed a baseball song, held up a rookie's stumbling feet
Is the saddest sight when it's left alone that ever your eyes could meet.

So whenever I go to Flatbush with the help of the BMT
I never walk by the empty park without pausing in hopes I won't see
A park standing there, empty and barren, with some seats falling apart
'Cause I can't help thinking the poor old park is a park with a broken heart.*

*From *Wake Up the Echoes,* ed. Bob Cooke, Hanover House, 1956. Reprinted by permission.

Although it is not discernible in the picture, the wrecker's ball was painted to look like a baseball. Nothing, however, could lighten the mood of those present on February 23, 1960, when the demolition of Ebbets Field was begun. There would never be another ball park quite like it. *Wide World Photos*

CHAPTER TEN

1954

The Giants Take It All

The long season boiled down to a pair of three-game series during the first week of September; the first between the Indians and the Yankees, the second matching the Giants and the Dodgers—six crucial games in six days. There had not been a week like it since the 1951 play-off.

Cleveland arrived in New York with a four-and-a-half-game lead over the Yankees, having refused to fold in the latter stages of the season as had so many previous pretenders to the Yankee throne. They won twenty-six games in August, matched a ten-game New York winning streak with a nine-game streak of their own, and appeared to be a team without a weakness. Ready for the Yankee series were Early Wynn, Mike Garcia, and Bob Lemon, a powerful trio of right-handed pitchers enjoying a banner season.

Nearly 60,000 fans turned out for the opener, and sat glumly while Wynn methodically burned down the Yankees. He didn't allow a hit until the seventh, when Irv Noren's homer cut the Cleveland lead to 2–1, but Dave Philley answered that shot with a three-run homer in the top of the eighth that capped a four-run rally and extended the Indian lead to five and a half games.

Eddie Lopat, who practically owned the Indians, beat them the next day, 4–1, helped by Yogi Berra's two-run homer in the sixth. And the Bombers won the third game behind Whitey Ford and a Mickey Mantle homer, as well as Noren's spectacular catch in the eighth that stole a two-run homer from Hank Majeski. In the clubhouse after the game Casey Stengel put his feet on his desk and announced, "We're back in business!"

But the effort seemed to exhaust the Bombers. Cleveland regained the winning touch over the next ten days, while the Yankees stumbled. On September 12 the New Yorkers were six and a half games behind and in Cleveland for a doubleheader. Ninety thousand watched and roared as the Indians swept the Yanks and locked up the pennant. Bob Lemon won the first game, 4–1, for his twenty-second victory, and Early Wynn captured his twenty-first win in the nightcap, 3–2, after surrendering a two-run homer to Berra in the first inning. The largest crowd in baseball history joined the Cleveland players in loudly heckling the Yankees as the teams left the field.

The Yanks finished the season with 103 victories, the most Casey Stengel would ever win, but were still eight games behind the rampaging Indians.

It's possible that Hoyt Wilhelm, on the left, is still pitching somewhere. He holds the all-time major-league record for games played. In 1954 he led Giant relievers with a 12–4 record, and his 2.10 ERA led the National League. With him is Al Worthington, a relief pitcher, whom the Giants converted into a starter with modest results. *N.Y. Daily News Photo*

Coincidental with the first pennant loss in five years was the passing of several old favorites. Vic Raschi was traded during spring training after a salary dispute with George Weiss. He went to the Cardinals and on April 23 threw a fast ball to a Milwaukee Braves rookie named Henry Aaron, who hit it for the first home run of his career. Allie Reynolds said at the end of the season that he doubted if he'd be returning, and Gene Woodling was traded to the Orioles for Bob Turley and Don Larsen. Billy Martin was in the Army and Phil Rizzuto's .195 average foreshadowed the end of his career. Despite all these factors the Yankees were still good enough to beat anything short of a phenomenal performance.

The decisive Giant-Dodger clash took place at the Polo Grounds, with the Giants ahead in the standings by three games. The Dodgers took a 4–2 lead in the opener and knocked Sal Maglie out of the box, but the Durochermen tied the score in the sixth, and reliever Hoyt Wilhelm singled home the tie breaker in the seventh. Wilhelm pitched shutout ball over the last three innings and got credit for the 7–4 victory.

The Giants broke fast the next afternoon and grabbed a 4–1 lead, but Jim Gilliam's two-run homer in the seventh cut the lead to one. In the bottom of the seventh the Giants struck for seven runs, the last four crossing on Hank Thompson's grand slam. The New Yorkers won, 13–4, for twenty runs and twenty-six hits in two days, and in the clubhouse a merry Leo Durocher said, "Things are looking better every day!"

The Dodgers managed to salvage the third game, but then dropped a Labor Day doubleheader to the last-place Pittsburgh Pirates. The Giants maintained a comfortable lead until September 20, when Sal Maglie took the mound at Ebbets Field and beat the Dodgers, 7–1, for the pennant clincher. A morose Dodger fan muttered as he left the ball park, "They shoulda not let go Dressen."

On June 15, 1954, Hank Thompson belted a three-run homer with two out in the last of the ninth inning to beat the Cincinnati Reds, 5–3, and give the Giants a lead in the National League pennant race they never relinquished. Only Mays had more homers for the Giants that year than Thompson. *N.Y. Daily News Photo*

The new Brooklyn manager, Walter "Smokey" Alston, who in eight years of managing Dodger farm clubs never finished lower than third, inherited a club with a spotty pitching staff and an attack weakened by a season-long hand injury to Roy Campanella. Carl Erskine won eighteen games but dropped fifteen, and Don Newcombe's first year back from the Army was a 9–8 flop. Duke Snider and Gil Hodges wore out National League hurlers, but Campy's incapacitation hurt the team badly. Most of all, the Dodgers seemed to lack the kind of spark provided by a unique ballplayer, a player who could lift a team and inspire it with confidence.

A player like Willie Mays. Willie returned from the Army in time for most of the spring-training schedule. On opening day against the Dodgers at the Polo Grounds he crashed a mighty homer into the upper left-field deck that won the game for the Giants, 4–3. He continued to belt the ball out of reach through the first half of the season, and at the All Star break had thirty-one homers, ten better than Babe Ruth's 1927 pace. During the last week of June, Willie slammed six home runs while the Giants were finishing the month

The Sal Maglie Giant fans knew and loved. This picture was taken on September 20, the day Maglie beat the Dodgers, 7–1, at Ebbets Field and clinched the pennant for the Giants. *Yale Joel*, TIME/*Life Picture Agency* © TIME *Inc.*

In the Giants' clubhouse after the 1954 pennant clinching. Left to right: Dodger president Walter O'Malley, managers Leo Durocher and Walt Alston, and Giant president Horace Stoneham. *N.Y. Daily News Photo*

with a 25 and 4 mark. The Polo Grounders swept a pair of three-game series with the Dodgers just before the All Star game, and after June 15 were never out of first place.

Willie was indispensable, but the Giants could not have won without strong and consistent pitching. Sal Maglie's back troubles cleared up, and he contributed fourteen wins. Ruben Gomez had a record of 17–9 and a 2.88 ERA. Hoyt Wilhelm and Marv Grissom combined for twenty-two wins and twenty-six saves. But the critical difference was a young left-hander named Johnny Antonelli, one of the first "bonus babies," who received $65,000 to sign with the Braves in 1948. The Giants traded Bobby Thomson to Milwaukee in order to get Antonelli, but it was worth it. The graceful southpaw won twenty-one games, led the league in strikeouts and winning percentage, and had the best ERA among major-league starting pitchers: 2.30. Antonelli's performance made Larry Jansen's midseason retirement less damaging.

Had they been playing in the American League, however, the Giants would have finished fourteen games behind the Indians. Even with Willie Mays and Don Mueller, who finished one-two in the National League batting championship, the Giants seemed no match for Bobby Avila, the American League batting champ, Larry Doby, who led his league in homers and RBIs, and Al Rosen and Vic Wertz, a pair of dependable long-ball hitters.

But everyone agreed that the decisive Series edge was held by the Cleveland pitchers. As good as the hitters were, the 1954 Cleveland Indians are remembered for one of the most awesome pitching staffs in the history of the game. Wynn, Lemon, and Garcia combined for sixty-five wins, and Art Houtteman and Bob Feller won twenty-eight more between them. The bullpen crew, led by Don Mossi and Ray Narleski, wasn't needed too often, but when called upon gave a masterly performance. These hurlers led the Indians to 111 wins, the most in either league in almost half a century, and helped establish the Tribe as 8–5 favorites to win the World Series.

Don Mueller's magical ability to hit baseballs just beyond the reach of the opposition earned him the nickname "Mandrake." He had his best year in 1954 with 212 hits, and his .342 average was second to Willie Mays' .345 in the race for the batting title. In this picture he has just homered against the Dodgers. *UPI Photo*

The Giants' starting lineup before the first game of the 1954 World Series with the Cleveland Indians. First base, Whitey Lockman; second base, Davey Williams; third base, Hank Thompson; shortstop, Alvin Dark; right field, Don Mueller; center field, Willie Mays; left field, Monte Irvin; and catcher, Wes Westrum. The starting pitcher was Sal Maglie. *N.Y. Daily News Photo*

Unlikely heroes have a way of emerging in World Series play, but a more unlikely one than James Lamar "Dusty" Rhodes would have been difficult to imagine. He joined the Giants in 1952, a husky, cheerful man with a folksy Alabama drawl, impressive hitting talent, and all the fielding agility of a grizzly bear. In 1954 he hit fifteen homers and drove in fifty runs in just 164 official at bats. He hit .333 as a pinch hitter, and it was in this role that he almost completely dominated the 1954 Series.

The opening game, played before a capacity crowd at the Polo Grounds, began predictably with the Indians scoring twice in the first inning. But the Giants tied the score in the last of the third, and then Bob Lemon and Sal Maglie settled down and looked stronger with each successive scoreless inning. In the eighth the first two Cleveland hitters reached base, and southpaw Don Liddle was brought on to face Vic Wertz, whose triple in the first inning had produced the Indians' runs. Wertz pounded Liddle's first pitch on a line to deep center field that sent Willie Mays off on a frantic and seemingly futile dash. But when the ball finally began to drop, there was Willie, his back to the plate, arms straining, and stride weaving as he ran full tilt and watched the ball over his shoulder at the same time. He caught Wertz's drive at the warning track, spun out of his cap, and rifled the ball back to the infield in time to keep the runners from advancing. Marv Grissom relieved Liddle and got the last two outs of the inning.

In the top of the eighth inning of the first game of the 1954 World Series, Willie Mays, the National League's Most Valuable Player that season, made this unforgettable catch to rob Vic Wertz of a two-run triple. It prevented the Indians from breaking a 2–2 tie and forced the game into extra innings. *N.Y. Daily News Photo*

In 1954, Dusty Rhodes appeared in eighty-two games and hit .341. In this picture, taken before the opening game of the 1954 Series, he is selecting a bat in hopes of being called on to pinch-hit. His hopes were realized in the last of the tenth inning. *N.Y. Daily News Photo*

Then Dusty Rhodes took charge. In the last of the tenth, with runners on first and second, he pinch-hit for Monte Irvin and lifted Lemon's second pitch high down the right-field line. Tribe outfielder Dave Pope cruised back under the ball confidently, and then suddenly found himself pressed against the wall, only 260 feet from the plate. Rhodes' hit landed in the first row of seats, then bounced out and fell prankishly at Pope's feet. Lemon stared unbelievingly at the winning runs bounding across home plate, then flung his glove into the air and stalked to the clubhouse.

September 29, 1954

CLEVELAND

	ab	r	h	o	a
Smith, lf	4	1	1	1	0
Avila, 2b	5	1	1	2	3
Doby, cf	3	0	1	3	0
Rosen, 3b	5	0	1	1	3
Wertz, 1b	5	0	4	11	1
d Regalado	0	0	0	0	0
Grasso, c	0	0	0	1	0
Philley, rf	3	0	0	0	0
a Majeski	0	0	0	0	0
b Mitchell	0	0	0	0	0
Strickland, ss	3	0	0	2	3
Dente, ss	0	0	0	0	0
c Pope, rf	1	0	0	0	0
d Hegan, c	4	0	0	6	1
e Glynn, 1b	1	0	0	0	0
d Lemon, p	4	0	0	1	1
Total	38	2	8	x28	12

NEW YORK

	ab	r	h	o	a
Lockman, 1b	5	1	1	9	0
Dark, ss	4	0	2	3	2
Mueller, rf	5	1	2	2	0
Mays, cf	3	1	0	2	0
Thompson, 3b	3	1	1	3	3
Irvin, lf	3	0	0	5	0
f Rhodes	1	1	1	0	0
Williams, 2b	4	0	0	1	1
Westrum, c	4	0	2	5	0
Maglie, p	3	0	0	0	2
Liddle, p	0	0	0	0	0
Grissom, p	1	0	0	0	0
Total	36	5	9	30	8

a Announced as batter for Philley in eighth.
b Walked for Majeski in eighth.
c Called out on strikes for Strickland in eighth.
d Ran for Wertz in tenth.
e Struck out for Hegan in tenth.
f Homered for Irvin in tenth.
x One out when winning run scored.

```
Cleveland   2 0 0 0 0 0 0 0 0 0—2
New York    0 0 2 0 0 0 0 0 0 3—5
```

Errors—Mueller 2, Irvin. Runs batted in—Wertz 2, Mueller, Thompson, Rhodes 3. Two-base hit—Wertz. Three-base hit—Wertz. Home run—Rhodes. Stolen base—Mays. Sacrifices—Irvin, Dente. Left on base—Cleveland 13, New York 9. Bases on balls—Lemon 5, Maglie 2, Grissom 3. Struck out—Maglie 2, Grissom 2, Lemon 6. Hits off—Maglie 7 in 7 (none out in 8th), Liddle 0 in 1/3, Grissom 1 in 2 2/3. Runs and earned runs—Maglie 2 and 2, Lemon 5 and 5. Hit by pitcher—by Maglie (Smith). Wild pitch—Lemon. Winner—Grissom. Loser—Lemon. Umpires—Barlick (N), Berry (A), Conlan (N), Stevens (A), Warneke (N), Napp (A). Time—3:11. Attendance—52,751.

The next day the Cleveland lead-off hitter, Al Smith, smacked Johnny Antonelli's first pitch into the seats, but this advantage lasted only long enough for the Giants to call on Rhodes again. He pinch-hit for Irvin in the fifth with

Dusty Rhodes rounds first while Cleveland right fielder Dave Pope leaps in vain for Rhodes' fly ball that has just plopped into the stands no more than 258 feet from the plate. Indian hurler Bob Lemon stands helplessly on the mound. The Giants won, 5–2, and the Tribe never really recovered. *N.Y. Daily News Photo*

runners on first and third, and was sent sprawling by an Early Wynn fast ball aimed to discourage further heroics. But Dusty got up and stroked the next pitch into center field to bring in the tying run. The Giants went ahead moments later, and in the last of the eighth Rhodes supplied an insurance run with a home run onto the right field roof. The Giants won, 3–1, and departed for Cleveland in justifiably high spirits.

The third game was played in Cleveland's Municipal Stadium, but neither the home park nor the home crowd could change the Tribe's luck. The Giants treated Mike Garcia as disrespectfully as they had Lemon and Wynn, scored a run in the first inning, and then loaded the bases in the third. Monte Irvin

Johnny Antonelli, the southpaw ace of the Giants in 1954, pitching in the second game of the 1954 World Series. His record that season was 21–7, he finished with an ERA of 2.30, and he led the National League in shutouts. He capped his brilliant season with a 3–1 win in the second Series game and a save in the fourth contest. *N.Y. Daily News Photo*

was the scheduled hitter, but once again Dusty Rhodes was announced to pinch-hit. The Colossus of Rhodes, as dubbed by the *Times*' Arthur Daley, rapped a single to right to give the Giants a 3–0 lead. It was Dusty's third pinch hit, tying a record set by the Yankees' Bobby Brown in the seven-game 1947 Series. The Polo Grounders later added three more runs and won, 6–2. Ruben Gomez, with help from Wilhelm, was the winning pitcher.

With elimination imminent, Cleveland manager Al Lopez had no choice but to start Bob Lemon again, with only two days' rest. This decision denied Bob Feller his last chance to win a World Series game. Durocher felt he could gamble with Don Liddle, but at that point the Indians were so sluggish that Horace Stoneham might have looked good pitching against them. Two Tribe errors resulted in two Giant runs in the second inning, Mays doubled home another in the third, and Lemon failed to survive the fifth, when the Polo Grounders loaded the bases with none out. Hal Newhouser relieved and walked in the fourth run, and then Monte Irvin, finally given a chance to hit with runners on, singled home two more. The seventh run was registered moments later, and although Cleveland came up with four runs, their best effort of the Series, they were never really in the game. The final score was 7–4.

Dusty Rhodes wrecked Cleveland in the second game of the 1954 Series with a pinch single that tied the game and a towering home run that provided a valuable insurance tally. Here he is seen being congratulated by Chris Durocher, the Giant manager's son. *N.Y. Daily News Photo*

The 1954 World Champions. The bat boy is Bobby Weinstein. Front row, left to right: Johnny Antonelli, Sal Maglie, Whitey Lockman, coaches Larry Jansen and Fred Fitzsimmons, Eddie Brannick, manager Leo Durocher, coaches Frank Shellenback and Herman Franks, Davey Williams, Hank Thompson, and team physician Dr. Anthony Palermo. Second row, left to right: custodian Eddie Logan, Hoyt Wilhelm, Dusty Rhodes, Willie Mays, Don Mueller, Alvin Dark, Monte Irvin, Bill Taylor, Bobby Hofman, Joe Garagiola, Ruben Gomez, and trainer Frank Bowman. Third row, left to right: Paul Giel, Joe Amalfitano, Don Liddle, Bill Gardner, Al Worthington, Foster Castleman, John McCall, Alex Konikowski, Al Corwin, Marv Grissom, Ray Katt, Daryl Spencer, Wes Westrum, and Jim Hearn. *Brown Brothers*

It was the first National League sweep in the World Series since 1914, and the Giants' first world championship since 1933. Giant fans, not the least disappointed that the Series hadn't returned to the Polo Grounds, assembled at La Guardia airport and loudly welcomed their heroes on their return.

Cleveland fans had reason to mourn the breakdown of their pitching staff, but a glance at the hitting statistics is even more indicative of the Indians' failure. The Tribe stranded twenty-six runners in the first two games, and finished with a team batting average of .190. Their regular season leaders, Doby, Avila, and Rosen, contributed .125, .133, and .250, respectively, compared to .412 for Al Dark, .389 for Don Mueller, and .364 for Hank Thompson. Rhodes was not needed in the fourth game and finished with a gaudy Series average of .667. He was an easy winner of the classic's Most Valuable Player award.

At La Guardia, someone asked Durocher if he thought the Dodgers were tougher than the Indians.

"You can say that again!" shouted Leo.

Victory cigars and high spirits in the Champs' locker room. Seen here celebrating the Cleveland massacre are Joe Garagiola, second from left; Hoyt Wilhelm, in the background; Ray Katt, fifth from right; Johnny Antonelli, seated; and Davey Williams, on the far right. *UPI Photo*

CHAPTER ELEVEN

1955

The Woild Champs.
This IS Next Year!

The *Sporting News* predicted that the Milwaukee Braves would win the 1955 National League pennant. The Dodgers were given a good chance to edge out the Giants for second place. There was not a great deal of confidence in Alston expressed by baseball journalists, nor was there a conviction that Roy Campanella and Don Newcombe would return to previous form. The left side of the infield was also a question mark, owing to the disposal of the sure-handed Billy Cox. Spring-training events helped reinforce suspicions and pessimism. Alston announced that no job was assured, and proceeded to experiment with Peewee Reese in left field. He kept Jackie Robinson on the bench, used Campanella sparingly, and insisted that Don Newcombe take an occasional turn pitching batting practice.

The situation seemed ripe for mutiny, but on opening day Alston settled on a lineup that included Jackie Robinson at third, Sandy Amoros in left field, and the veterans in their accustomed places. By Memorial Day the pennant race was over. The Brooks won their first ten games in a row, to set a record for consecutive wins at the start of the season, dropped two to the Giants, and then won eleven more in succession. The eleventh was a 3–0 win over the Cubs in Chicago. Don Newcombe faced just twenty-seven batters in that game; the only man to hit safely was erased trying to steal. The Brooks won twenty-five of their first twenty-nine contests, and by the middle of May were in front by nine and a half games.

Don Newcombe, Duke Snider, and Walter O'Malley made sure the rest of the season was not uneventful. Newk went on a tear in the early going, and on July 31 his record stood at 18–2. He helped himself with a batting average close to .360, and when not pitching pinch-hit at a .381 clip. He tailed off in the last two months of the season, however, and won only two of his last seven starts. The Duke had his best season. Long past were his spells of brooding and petulance. He led the majors with 142 RBIs and 136 runs scored, and was high among National League leaders with forty-two homers and a .309 average. He was a complete ballplayer. O'Malley threw a wet blanket on the festive

Towering Don Newcombe was an awesome sight on the mound. He is seen here completing a one-hit shutout over the Chicago Cubs that capped an eleven-game Brooklyn win streak early in the 1955 campaign. The following year he won twenty-seven games and became the first winner of the Cy Young award. *Francis Miller,* TIME*/Life Picture Agency* © TIME *Inc.*

In addition to his twenty wins in 1955, Don Newcombe hit seven home runs and drove in twenty-three runs. In twenty-one pinch-hit appearances his batting average was .381. He would frequently bat higher in the lineup than the ninth spot traditionally reserved for pitchers. *N.Y. Daily News Photo*

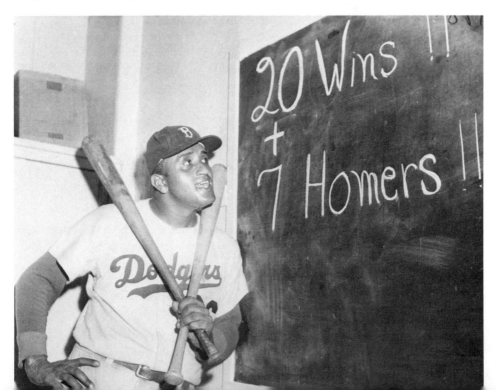

The Duke. He had his best all-round season in 1955, with forty-two homers, a league-leading total of 136 RBIs, and a .309 batting average. He added four home runs in the Dodgers' triumphant World Series. In eighteen seasons his lifetime batting average was .295. *John Dominis,* TIME/*Life Picture Agency* © TIME *Inc.*

season by announcing that the Dodgers would play seven home games in Jersey City during the 1956 season. "I am a connoisseur of empty seats," he said, and quoted figures that showed a decline in Dodger attendance over the past nine years. He stated that he could not use Ebbets Field much longer, and hinted that the city had better help him with a new ball-park site or face the likelihood of the Dodgers' moving to a more accommodating municipality.

Despite these cheerless pronouncements, the Dodgers continued to win. On August 4 in Milwaukee they beat the Braves, 11–10, and took a fifteen-and-a-half-game lead. A little more than a month later the Dodgers were back in Milwaukee, and Jackie Robinson hit a home run to lead the Brooks to a 10–2 win and the pennant clincher.

Buried beneath the Brooklyn landslide were the defending World Champions, the luckless New York Giants. Everything went wrong for them in 1955. Johnny Antonelli and Sal Maglie both slumped, and quarreled with Leo Durocher, and before the summer was over Maglie was sold to the Cleveland

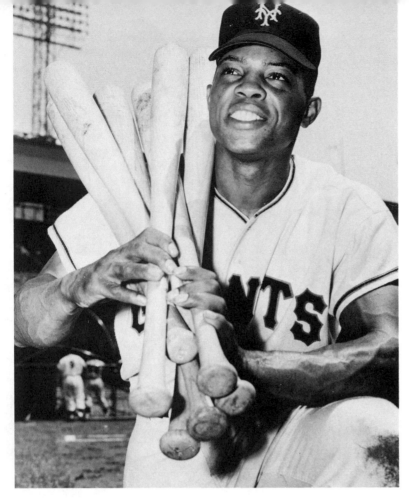

In his prime Willie Mays could hit the ball as hard as anyone who ever played the game. His powerful wrists and shoulders drove out a league-leading total of fifty-one homers in 1955; ten years later he led the league with fifty-two. Only two men have hit more home runs in their lifetime than Willie's total of 660. *UPI Photo*

Indians. Alvin Dark and Davey Williams were injured for most of the season, and Monte Irvin was sent down to the Giants' farm team in Minneapolis. Only the thundering bat of Willie Mays prevented a total collapse. His fifty-one home runs led both leagues, and his threat to Babe Ruth's single-season home-run record drew otherwise disenchanted patrons to the Polo Grounds. Durocher quit at the end of the season, and Horace Stoneham named Bill Rigney as Leo's successor. At the same time Stoneham was paying close attention to the machinations of Walter O'Malley.

"You won't ever see a fellow with hardly more than two years' experience who is as good for knowing how to play this game in all its many particulars." This was vintage Stengelese, and on this occasion in praise of young Bobby Richardson, who had been called up from Denver to help out in the Yankee infield. Richardson joined other first-year Yankees who would contribute to Bomber successes in the 1960s: Bob Turley, Bill "Moose" Skowron, and the Yankees' first black player, Elston Howard.

The new men performed capably, but the team depended on Yogi Berra and Mickey Mantle, both of whom came through handsomely in 1955 with a total of sixty-four homers and 207 RBIs. As usual, Yogi was at his best under pressure. On September 16 the Red Sox, who, along with the Indians and

White Sox, had been crowding the Yankees all season, visited Yankee Stadium. A victory would give the Yanks a two-game advantage in the loss column over the second-place Indians, the first breathing space of the summer. Berra's home run in the sixth helped provide a 3–1 lead, but the Red Sox came back with three runs in the eighth. In the last of the ninth Boston reliever Ellis Kinder got the first out, then Hank Bauer lofted a homer into the Red Sox bullpen to tie the score at 4–4. After Gil McDougald popped out, Yogi whacked Kinder's first pitch into the seats for the game winner. Berra was subsequently named the American League's Most Valuable Player for the second year in a row and the third time in five years.

Five days later the Yankees won their eighth straight game, and the next day beat the Red Sox in the second game of a day-night doubleheader to clinch the pennant. In early August, Stengel predicted that it would take an eight-game winning streak for one of the contenders to pull away. Before the season began he said that ninety-five wins would take the flag. The Yankee pennant clincher in Boston was their ninety-fifth victory. Asked to comment on the Dodgers' impressive showing, Casey ventured another forecast: "Don't worry, the Yankees always take care of the Series."

Yogi Berra won the American League's Most Valuable Player award three times: in 1951, 1954, and 1955. His awkward but lethal batting style produced 358 homers, the present record for catchers. He holds the record for World Series appearances: seventy-five games, nearly half a season. *N.Y. Daily News Photo*

Left: Whitey Ford's graceful pitching motion, seen here in the opening game of the 1955 World Series against the Dodgers at Yankee Stadium. He won two of the three Yankee victories in that Series, and holds eight career World Series records for pitchers. For sixteen seasons he was the Yankees' "money" pitcher. *N.Y. Daily News Photo   Right:* Tommy Byrne enjoyed a fine comeback season in 1955, with a 16–5 record after four years of obscurity. He won the second game of the 1955 World Series, and was the only southpaw to pitch a complete game victory over the Dodgers during the 1955 season. *N.Y. Daily News Photo*

Sure enough, the Series began with a pattern grimly familiar to Brooklyn rooters. At Yankee Stadium the Yankees won the first two games, 6–5 and 4–2. In the opener Joe Collins homered twice, and Whitey Ford, with ninth-inning help from Bob Grim, held on for the victory. Jackie Robinson stole home in the eighth, his eighteenth career theft of home. The Dodgers' ace Don Newcombe, pitching in his first World Series game since the opener of the 1949 match, was knocked out of the box in the sixth inning. The second game was a sweet triumph for Tommy Byrne, who had a comeback 16–5 season for the Yankees in 1955. He bounced from the Browns to the White Sox to the Senators after the Bombers released him in 1951, rejoined the Yanks in 1954, and a year later won his first World Series game. He gave up five hits and drove home the Yankees' third and fourth runs with a single in the fourth inning. As the classic moved to Brooklyn, it was pointed out that no team had ever lost the first two games of a World Series and gone on to win the championship.

Just moments after Yogi Berra helped Gil Hodges remove a piece of dirt from his eye, the Brooklyn first baseman belted a two-run homer that helped the Dodgers win the fourth World Series game and gain a 2–2 tie in games. *N.Y. Daily News Photo*

But back at Ebbets Field the Dodgers finally unleashed their attack and evened the Series with 8–3 and 8–5 victories. Roy Campanella clouted two homers, Gil Hodges and Duke Snider each connected once, and Carl Furillo, Sandy Amoros, and Jim Gilliam all produced run-scoring hits. Johnny Podres celebrated his twenty-third birthday with a complete game victory in the third game, and Carl Erskine, Don Bessent, and Clem Labine joined forces to win the fourth contest. In that game Yankee co-owner Del Webb was conked on the head by a pop fly and had to retire to the clubhouse for ice-pack treatment. He was soon joined by several Yankee pitchers. In the third and fourth games Stengel used nine hurlers in an effort to stop the Dodgers.

This set the stage for Don Newcombe to redeem himself with a win that would give the Brooks the Series lead. But Alston's confidence in the big man was badly shaken. The nod went instead to a skinny rookie named Roger Craig, who the year before had been pitching in the Class B Piedmont League. He pitched six strong innings before needing help from Labine in the seventh, but at that point the Dodgers were leading, 4–2, on a two-run homer by Amoros and a pair of bases-empty home runs by Snider. Both teams scored a run in the eighth, but Labine set down the Yanks in the ninth to preserve Craig's victory. As the Yankees packed up to move back to Yankee Stadium, Hank Bauer muttered, "I'll be glad to get out of this rat trap."

In deference to Ebbets Field's ruinous effect on visiting southpaws, Casey Stengel kept Whitey Ford safely on the bench during the Brooklyn battles. With four days' rest, Ford was virtually untouchable. He went all the way in the sixth game, and gave up just one run and four hits. The Yankees scored all their runs in a five-run first inning, a rally capped by Bill Skowron's three-run homer. The Series was tied at three games apiece.

Seven times previously the Dodgers had failed to capture the World Series; the last five attempts had been thwarted by the Yankees. Johnny Podres, the Dodgers' seventh-game starter, had failed to finish his last thirteen regular season starts. Tommy Byrne was the Yankee starting pitcher, and as he breezed through three hitless innings, hearts began to sink all over Brooklyn. But Byrne's spell was broken in the top of the fourth, when Roy Campanella doubled down the third-base line. Gil Hodges scored Campy with a single, and in the sixth Hodges gave the Brooks a 2–0 lead with a sacrifice fly. Meanwhile, Podres was keeping the Bombers at bay with his looping curve ball, teasing change-up, and a sneaky fast ball he hadn't shown often at Ebbets Field. In the sixth Alston sent George Shuba in to hit for second baseman Don Zimmer in an effort to increase the lead. Shuba was retired, but what happened next was far more significant. Jim Gilliam came in from left to replace Zimmer, and Sandy Amoros replaced Gilliam.

In the last of the sixth the Yankees moved runners to first and second with no outs. Yogi Berra came up next, and the Stadium crowd began to buzz with anticipation. Seconds later everyone was up and roaring as Yogi sliced a drive down the left-field line that looked good for extra bases and a tie game. But the fleet Amoros flashed over, lunged for the ball, and caught it. He then skidded to a stop, turned, and whipped the ball back to the infield in time to double McDougald off first and break the back of the Yankee rally. It was a remarkable catch, and a grab only a left-hander could have made—a rightie wouldn't have reached the ball backhanded—and even more admirable when it is recalled how challenging even routine fly balls could be in Yankee Stadium's left field during early autumn.

Podres snuffed out another Yankee rally in the eighth, and in the last of the ninth retired the first two Yankee hitters. The multitudes watching and listening held their breath as Elston Howard came to the plate. Howard hit a grounder to Peewee Reese, the only Dodger dating back to Brooklyn's first World Series loss to the Yankees in 1941. Peewee scooped the ball up, flipped to Hodges, and all hell broke loose.

Johnny Podres pitching in the seventh game of the 1955 World Series at Yankee Stadium. Podres had his best seasons with the Los Angeles Dodgers, but his seventh-game victory in the 1955 Series made him a Brooklyn legend. *N.Y. Daily News Photo*

Sandy Amoros robbing Yogi Berra of an extra-base hit in the sixth inning of the final game of the 1955 World Series. Amoros whirled and doubled a Yankee runner off first base, to check a Bomber rally and preserve Podres' victory. *N.Y. Daily News Photo*

October 4, 1955

BROOKLYN	ab	r	h	o	a
Gilliam, lf-2b	4	0	1	2	0
Reese, ss	4	1	1	2	6
Snider, cf	3	0	0	2	0
Campanella, c	3	1	1	5	0
Furillo, rf	3	0	0	3	0
Hodges, lb	2	0	1	10	0
Hoak, 3b	3	0	1	1	1
Zimmer, 2b	2	0	0	0	2
aShuba	1	0	0	0	0
Amoros, lf	0	0	0	2	1
Podres, p	4	0	0	0	1
Total	29	2	5	27	11

NEW YORK	ab	r	h	o	a
Rizzuto, ss	3	0	1	1	3
Martin, 2b	3	0	1	1	6
McDougald, 3b	4	0	3	1	1
Berra, c	4	0	1	4	1
Bauer, rf	4	0	0	1	0
Skowron, lb	4	0	1	11	1
Cerv, cf	4	0	0	5	0
Howard, lf	4	0	1	2	0
Byrne, p	2	0	0	0	2
Grim, p	0	0	0	1	0
bMantle	1	0	0	0	0
Turley, p	0	0	0	0	0
Total	33	0	8	27	14

aGrounded out for Zimmer in sixth.
bPopped out for Grim in seventh.

```
Brooklyn   0 0 0 1 0 1 0 0 0–2
New York   0 0 0 0 0 0 0 0 0–0
```

Error—Skowron. Runs batted in—Hodges 2. Two-base hits—Skowron, Campanella, Berra. Sacrifices—Snider, Campanella. Sacrifice fly—Hodges. Double play—Amoros, Reese, and Hodges. Left on base—Brooklyn 8, New York 8. Bases on balls—Byrne 3, Grim 1, Turley 1, Podres 2. Struck out—Byrne 2, Grim 1, Turley 1, Podres 4. Hits off—Byrne 3 in 5 1/3, Grim 1 in 1 2/3, Turley 1 in 2. Runs and earned runs—Byrne 2–1, Grim 0–0, Turley 0–0, Podres 0–0. Wild pitch—Grim. Loser—Byrne. Umpires—Honochick (A) plate, Dascoli (N) first base, Summers (A) second base, Ballanfant (N) third base, Flaherty (A) left field, Donatelli (N) right field. Time—2:44. Attendance—62,465.

Horn-blowing motorcades sped through Brooklyn, sirens wailed, church bells pealed, firecrackers exploded, blizzards of confetti swirled from office windows, total strangers embraced and danced in the streets, and stuffed dummies with "Yankees" scrawled across their chests dangled from lampposts. Joseph Saden, proprietor of Joe's Delicatessen at 324 Utica Avenue, set up a sidewalk stand and gave away hot dogs. Borough President John Cashmore sermonized that "the Dodgers must never leave Brooklyn!" Like a hundred New Year's Eves rolled into one, the rejoicing continued far into the night. At long last the Brooklyn Dodgers were World Champions and, to make the moment perfect, their victims had been the hated Yankees, the team that had denied Brooklyn the grail so many times.

The first and last Brooklyn Dodgers team to win the world championship. The bat boy is Charley DiGiovanna. Front row, left to right: George Shuba, Don Zimmer, coaches Joe Becker and Jake Pitler, manager Walt Alston, coach Babe Herman, Peewee Reese, Dixie Howell, Sandy Amoros, and Roy Campanella. Second row, left to right: clubhouse man John Griffin, Carl Erskine, Sandy Koufax, travel secretary Lee Scott, Roger Craig, Don Newcombe, Karl Spooner, Don Hoak, Carl Furillo, Frank Kellert, and trainer Dr. Harold Wendler. Third row, left to right: Russ Meyer, Jim Gilliam, Billy Loes, Clem Labine, Gil Hodges, Ed Roebuck, Don Bessent, Duke Snider, Johnny Podres, Al Walker, and Jackie Robinson. *Brown Brothers*

October 5, 1955, the moment Brooklyn fans had dreamed of for three generations: the winning of a world championship. Johnny Podres has just beaten the Yankees, 2–0, in the seventh game of the 1955 Series. Roy Campanella and Don Hoak rush to embrace their triumphant hurler. *N.Y. Daily News Photo*

CHAPTER TWELVE

1956

The Last Subway Series

While Dodger fans savored their championship, Walter O'Malley continued to press his demands for a new stadium location. In February, Mayor Robert Wagner introduced a Sports Center Authority bill into the state legislature that would provide a building site at the Flatbush terminus of the Long Island Railroad. But passage was blocked by upstate legislators, who charged favoritism and argued that comparatively few New York State citizens would benefit from such an allocation. As the bill foundered, O'Malley grew restive.

More pressure was applied by Horace Stoneham, who said that if the Dodgers moved, the Giants would have to relocate as well. Stoneham said that the eleven home games with the Dodgers accounted for one-third of the Giants' annual revenues. He also pointed to the football Giants' decision to play future home games at Yankee Stadium as evidence of the Polo Grounds' declining suitability.

Meanwhile events at Yankee Stadium were proceeding routinely. The Bombers got off to a fast start, and an eleven-game winning streak in July gave them a first-place lead of ten and a half games. An otherwise uneventful campaign was enlivened by Mickey Mantle's pursuit of Babe Ruth's single-season home-run record. The Mick belted two homers on opening day and by the end of May had twenty home runs, fifty runs batted in, and an average of .425. This pace slackened as the season progressed, but as late as August 25 Mantle, with forty-four homers, was still four ahead of the record.

As had many sluggers before him, Mantle failed to match Ruth's September home-run output. He hit his fiftieth on September 18, the day the Yanks clinched the pennant. That particular blast slammed into Comiskey Park's upper deck with such force that Casey Stengel was moved to say, "Seats were flyin' around for five minutes!" Mickey finished the season with fifty-two home runs, 130 RBIs, and a .353 average. He became the seventh American League player to win the triple crown since the turn of the century, and also won the Most Valuable Player award.

Amid the celebrations of Mantle's achievements and the Yankee pennant victory, a familiar figure was noticeably absent. After thirteen seasons and more than 1,600 games as the Yankee shortstop, Phil Rizzuto was unceremoniously released by the Yankees in late August. The move enabled the

The next-to-last season at Ebbets Field began happily with the raising of the world-championship flag. Peewee Reese, on the left, and manager Walt Alston, behind flag, help with the ceremony. *N.Y. Daily News Photo*

Bombers to make room for Enos Slaughter, who had been purchased from Kansas City. When asked how he felt about joining the New Yorkers, Slaughter summed up certain attitudes toward the Yankee management by replying forthrightly, "I feel sick all over."

So did most Giant fans. Just two years after their championship season, the Polo Grounders skidded into sixth place, and finished only seven games better than the last-place Cubs. Willie Mays had only a mediocre year, for him, and the team's over-all batting average was the lowest in both leagues. A desperate management made a trade with the Cardinals that landed Red Schoendienst and Jackie Brandt for Al Dark and Whitey Lockman. At the same time supposedly precocious youngsters like Bill White, Daryl Spencer, and Foster Castleman were pressed into service. Nothing helped. Johnny Antonelli had a 20–13 season, but the next most productive hurlers were Ruben Gomez and Al Worthington, each of whom won seven games and combined to lose thirty-one. Gomez even succeeded in embarrassing himself and his teammates in a game against the Milwaukee Braves on July 18. He hit Joe Adcock with a pitched ball, and when the burly Brave advanced toward the mound, Ruben threw the ball at him again, and then ran full speed into the safety of his dugout.

Unusual spectacles were more the rule at Ebbets Field, and the 1956 season offered a number of them. On opening day an unprecedented event took place: the raising of the world-championship flag. The festivities were spoiled by the Phillies, who won the game, 8–6, but two days later the Brooks won their "opener" at Jersey City. In the gray and decaying former home of the Giants'

In 1956 Mickey Mantle made a run at Babe Ruth's single-season home-run record, and finished the season with league-leading totals in homers (52), RBIs (130), and batting (.353). His eighteen homers in World Series play is an all-time major-league record. *N.Y. Daily News Photo*

Triple A farm team the Dodgers beat the Phils, 5–4, while a not entirely partisan crowd alternately cheered and jeered the action.

A rare treat was supplied by Carl Erskine when he threw a no-hitter against the Giants at Ebbets Field on May 12. Spectacular defensive work by Jackie Robinson and Carl Furillo turned would-be base hits into outs, and in the top of the ninth Whitey Lockman hit a ball over the right-field screen that at the last second hooked foul by six inches.

But the most uncommon sight of all was Sal Maglie wearing a shirt that had "Dodgers" written across it. Early in the season the Dodgers played an exhibition game with the Cleveland Indians, and Maglie pitched four hitless innings for the Tribe. When Cleveland placed him on waivers two weeks later, the Brooks snapped Maglie up. The move paid immediate dividends. In his first start Sal shut out the Braves, and then went on to join Don Newcombe, Carl Erskine, and Roger Craig in forming the strongest starting rotation Brooklyn had employed in many years.

The Dodgers, Braves, and Cincinnati Reds staged a three-team race right down to the season's final weekend, and it was Maglie who, almost single-handed, kept the Brooks at or near the top in September. On the eleventh a 4–2 win over the Braves at Ebbets Field put the Dodgers in a tie for first. Sal

On May 12, 1956, Carl Erskine pitched his second career no-hitter, 3–0, over the Giants at Ebbets Field. This photo shows the action in the top of the ninth. Whitey Lockman hit this pitch over the right-field screen, foul by just a foot, then was retired for the last out. *N.Y. Daily News Photo*

went all the way in that game for his tenth win, and even drove in two runs with a sharp single. As he strode to the mound in the ninth, the Faithful gave Maglie a standing ovation. Five days later the Barber beat the Reds, 3–2, and the Dodgers took a half-game lead. And then on the twenty-fifth he embellished his spectacular comeback with a 5–0 no-hitter over the Phillies. He was thirty-nine years old and more than a year past the point where everyone had assumed he was washed up.

But the Braves were winning too, and with three games left in the season, they led the Dodgers by one. Three games between the Brooks and the Pirates at Ebbets Field and the Braves and Cardinals in St. Louis decided the pennant. Behind Maglie and Labine the Dodgers won their first two games, while the Braves obligingly dropped a pair to the Cards. As a result, on the season's final Sunday the Brooks were in first place by a game and could do no worse than tie. Duke Snider made sure there would be no play-off. He hit a three-run homer in the first inning off Vernon Law, and clubbed a two-run shot in the fifth for his forty-third home run of the season, a Dodger record. Then in the seventh he demonstrated his versatility with a leaping catch against the center-field wall that choked off a Pittsburgh rally. With an 8–6 victory, the Dodgers won the National League pennant.

Rested from their easy race and anxious to recapture the world title that had been residing in neighboring boroughs for two years, the Yankees invaded

Above: Just two years after he had beaten the Dodgers for the Giants' pennant clincher in 1954, Sal Maglie is given a hero's escort by the Dodgers after he pitched a no-hitter over the Phillies on September 25 to keep the Brooks in the thick of the pennant fight. On the left is Roy Campanella, on the right Don Drysdale and coach Jake Pitler. *Brown Brothers* *Left:* The strong right arm in the Brooklyn bullpen for ten seasons belonged to Clem Labine. In 1956 he appeared in sixty-two games, posted a 10–6 record, and led the league with nineteen saves. He had a win and a save in the 1955 Series and had a complete game, ten-inning victory in the sixth game of the 1956 World Series. *N.Y. Daily News Photo*

Ebbets Field and were flattened by Sal Maglie in the Series opener. The Barber gave up a two-run homer in the first to Mickey Mantle, but Brooklyn tied the score in the second and went ahead in the third on Gil Hodges' three-run wallop. The final score was 6–3. Maglie went the distance and struck out ten in his first World Series victory.

The second game was a pitcher's nightmare, as twenty-one runs and twenty-four hits rattled around the Bedford Avenue ball park. Don Newcombe was relieved after giving up a grand-slam homer to Yogi Berra in the second inning, but Dodger hitters responded with six runs in the bottom of the second, three crossing on Snider's homer high over the screen. Seven Yankee pitchers failed to contain the Dodgers, who went on to win, 13–8, in the longest nine-inning game in World Series history.

Dodger fans really didn't expect their team to sweep the Series, and so were not too disappointed when the Yankees won the third game at Yankee Stadium, 5–3. Brooklyn had a 2–1 lead going into the last of the sixth, but were done in by an ancient nemesis when forty-year-old Enos Slaughter drilled a three-run homer to give the Yanks a 4–2 lead. Each team scored once more, but Whitey Ford hung on for nine innings and didn't let the Dodgers catch up.

Home runs by Mickey Mantle and Hank Bauer helped win the fourth game, 6–2, and even the Series at two games apiece. Sixteen-game winner Tom Sturdivant pitched nine strong innings, while Carl Erskine, Ed Roebuck, and Don Drysdale worked artlessly for the Dodgers.

After dropping the first two games of the 1956 World Series to the Dodgers, the Yankees won the third game behind Enos Slaughter's three-run home run and Whitey Ford's route-going pitching performance. Slaughter was forty years old at the time; two years later he hit .304 in seventy-seven games for the Yankees. *N.Y. Daily News Photo*

Among the dozens of peerless hurlers to appear in World Series play, Donald James Larsen was surely the least likely to produce the classic's greatest pitching performance. In 1954 he had a 3–21 season with the Baltimore Orioles, and in 1956 his record with the Yankees was an ordinary 11–5. He started the second game of the 1956 Series and was knocked out in the second inning.

With these considerations in mind, Yankee fans greeted Larsen's fifth-game starting assignment warily. The tall right-hander began by easily retiring the Dodgers in the top of the first. In the second Jackie Robinson led off with a line drive that third baseman Andy Carey deflected toward shortstop Gil McDougald, whose throw to first barely nipped Robinson. The next eight Dodgers went down in order, and in the last of the fourth inning Mantle homered off Sal Maglie to give New York a 1–0 lead. In the top of the fifth Mickey robbed Gil Hodges of an extra-base hit with a running backhanded catch in deep center field. Sandy Amoros followed with a hard drive into the right-field seats that was foul by less than a foot.

The first pitch of the fifth 1956 World Series game. The Yankee pitcher Don Larsen is seen here throwing a strike past Brooklyn lead-off hitter Jim Gilliam. Gilliam was retired, as were the next twenty-six men to face Larsen. *N.Y. Daily News Photo*

The following photos illustrate how close the Dodgers came to ruining Larsen's perfect game. In the first sequence Jackie Robinson's hard grounder caroms off Andy Carey's glove into the hands of Gil McDougald, whose throw beats Robinson by a spike length. This action occurred in the second inning. *Wide World Photos*

In the last of the fifth inning Mickey Mantle snared this drive to rob Gil Hodges of an extra-base hit and preserve Larsen's masterpiece. At this point in his career Mantle had achieved fielding proficiency nearly equal to his hitting prowess. *N.Y. Daily News Photo*

From that point on it seemed as if Larsen had bewitched the Dodgers. Using the smooth and deliberate "no-windup" delivery that he had adopted earlier in the season when Stengel advised him that he was tipping off his pitches, Larsen set down one Brooklyn hitter after another. He didn't have overpowering stuff, but he put each pitch exactly where he wanted it and apparently where each batter least expected it. He got another run in the sixth and breezed through the seventh and eighth innings. The top of the ninth was played in an eerie silence that was broken by brief, nervous cheers following strikes and the first two outs. Larsen quickly got two strikes on pinch hitter Dale Mitchell, and then the excruciating tension was shattered when Larsen whipped a fast ball past Mitchell, plate umpire Babe Pinelli's right arm stabbed into the air, and the first no-hitter in World Series history and the first perfect game in thirty-four years was completed.

October 8, 1956

BROOKLYN	ab	r	h		NEW YORK	ab	r	h
Gilliam, 2b	3	0	0		Bauer, rf	4	0	1
Reese, ss	3	0	0		Collins, 1b	4	0	1
Snider, cf	3	0	0		Mantle, cf	3	1	1
Robinson, 3b	3	0	0		Berra, c	3	0	0
Hodges, 1b	3	0	0		Slaughter, lf	2	0	0
Amoros, lf	3	0	0		Martin, 2b	3	0	1
Furillo, rf	3	0	0		McDougald, ss	2	0	0
Campanella, c	3	0	0		Carey, 3b	3	1	1
Maglie, p	2	0	0		Larsen, p	2	0	0
a Mitchell	1	0	0					
Total	27	0	0		Total	26	2	5

aCalled out on strikes for Maglie in ninth.

```
Brooklyn    0  0  0  0  0  0  0  0  0—0
New York    0  0  0  1  0  1  0  0  x—2
```

Errors—None. Runs batted in—Mantle, Bauer. Home run—Mantle. Sacrifices—Larsen. Double plays—Reese and Hodges; Hodges, Campanella, Robinson; Campanella and Robinson. Left on base—Dodgers 0, Yankees 3. Bases on balls—Maglie 2. Struck out—Larsen 7, Maglie 5. Winner—Larsen. Loser—Maglie. Umpires—Pinelli (N), Soar (A), Boggess (N), Napp (A), Gorman (N), Runge (A). Time—2:06. Attendance—64,519.

Larsen made just ninety-seven pitches, got behind only nine hitters, and went to three and two on one batter. His feat was the talk of the city and he became an overnight celebrity. Dodger fans, of course, did not contribute to the felicitations, nor did Larsen's estranged wife, who petitioned to attach his World Series share.

Back at Ebbets Field for the sixth contest, more zeroes lit the scoreboard as Clem Labine and Bob Turley matched shutouts for nine innings. Labine retired the Yanks in the top of the tenth, and in the home half of the inning

Don Larsen has just completed a perfect game and the first no-hitter in World Series history. It gave the Yankees a three-to-two game edge in the 1956 Series against the Dodgers. Yogi Berra is the man embracing Larsen. *UPI Photo*

Jim Gilliam walked, was sacrificed to second, and scored the winning run when Jackie Robinson's line drive whistled over Enos Slaughter's head and rolled to the wall.

To that point the Series had followed exactly the same pattern as the 1955 classic, with each team winning its home games. And just as the Dodgers were able to overcome the Yankees' home advantage the year before in the seventh game, so did the Bombers upset their hosts in the deciding game of the 1956 Series. The game marked the final chapter in Don Newcombe's short and unhappy World Series career. During the regular season he had achieved a superb 27–7 record that earned him the Most Valuable Player trophy as well as the first annual Cy Young award. But in four and two-thirds innings of the 1956 Series he surrendered ten runs and eleven hits. Yogi Berra's grand slam ruined Newk in the second game, then Yogi hit a pair of two-run homers in the seventh contest that got the Yankees off to an early 4–0 lead and sent the crestfallen Newcombe to the clubhouse. Elston Howard's homer in the fourth made the score 5–0, and in the seventh a home run with the bases loaded by Bill Skowron removed any doubt as to where the world championship flag would fly in 1957. Johnny Kucks allowed just three hits in shutting out the Brooks, 9–0.

Besides Larsen, the big story was the Dodgers' inability to sustain the robust hitting that marked their opening victories. After collecting nineteen runs and twenty-one hits in the first two games, the Brooks could only manage six runs in the last five contests. At the same time Stengel used eleven pitchers in the first two Ebbets Field encounters, and then relaxed as Ford, Sturdivant, Larsen, Turley, and Kucks ran off five straight complete games.

In the sixth game of the 1956 Series, Clem Labine sat down on second base while Casey Stengel conferred with his pitcher Bob Turley. American League umpire Larry Napp told Labine to get up, and Labine stubbornly refused for a few moments. Gil McDougald is the bemused spectator. *N.Y. Daily News Photo*

The Yankees won the seventh game of the 1956 World Series at Ebbets Field, 9–0. The crusher came in the top of the seventh inning, when Bill "Moose" Skowron hit a grand-slam homer. His welcoming committee consisted of the bat boy, Elston Howard, and Yogi Berra. The disconsolate Dodger is Roy Campanella. *Brown Brothers*

CHAPTER THIRTEEN

1957

New York City: A Three-Time Loser

Jackie Robinson's baseball career ended as it had begun: amid an atmosphere of surprise, uncertainty, and controversy. On December 13, 1956, he was traded to the Giants for pitcher Dick Littlefield and an estimated $65,000 cash. Murray Waldman, a Giant fan from Little Neck, said, "First Durocher, now Robinson. How many enemies can we absorb?" Two years earlier the trade would have precipitated even more emphatic protests, but in late 1956 Giant and Dodger fans were a dispirited lot. Then in January, Jackie announced his retirement in an exclusive article for *Look* magazine. He said that he had made up his mind to retire before the trade but, because of his agreement with *Look,* was not able to inform the teams. A few writers criticized the manner and timing of his retirement announcement, prompting Robinson to call a press conference and angrily defend his intentions and actions. Despite his denials, there were many who felt that Jackie would have played another year for the Dodgers but had decided to retire rather than appear in a Giant uniform. In any event, when the season began Robinson was vice-president in charge of personnel relations for the Chock Full o' Nuts restaurant chain. He retired with a lifetime batting average of .311 and left behind vivid memories of spirited play and brash combativeness.

During the winter Walter O'Malley switched his sights from Brooklyn to Los Angeles, where legislators and developers were anxious to accommodate his every wish. O'Malley went through the motions of resolving the location issue in favor of Brooklyn, but his actions revealed his intentions. In January he bought a forty-four-passenger aircraft, and explained, "It would prove useful if the team decided to leave Brooklyn." Six weeks later he purchased Wrigley Field in Los Angeles and arranged for the transfer of the incumbent minor-league team. This latter action removed an important legal obstacle to establishing a major-league franchise in Los Angeles. O'Malley then sold Ebbets Field to a Brooklyn contractor, and even the most diehard of the Faithful knew that nothing could be done to save the Dodgers. Just before opening day O'Malley hired Emmett Kelly, the sad-faced clown, to perform at Ebbets Field before all home games.

The Dodgers were old, and Robinson's absence, as well as the transfer wrangles, burdened them additionally. The median age of Maglie, Reese, Campanella, Furillo, and Hodges was thirty-six, and before the end of the year Newcombe, Erskine, Labine, and Snider would be thirty-one. There was some life left in those old bodies, but not quite enough to bring Brooklyn a third consecutive pennant. Carl Furillo batted over .300 for the fifth time in his career, Duke Snider whacked forty homers, and Gil Hodges hit .299 and drove in ninety-eight runs. But Roy Campanella did not recover from nagging injuries, and Newcombe, Podres, and Maglie combined for just twenty-nine victories.

Even so, the Brooks stayed in the thick of a five-team pennant fight until mid-August, thanks mostly to the pitching of twenty-year-old Don Drysdale, a tall right-hander with a buggy-whip delivery and a sizzling fast ball. On July 15 the Phillies, Cardinals, Braves, Dodgers, and Reds were within two and a half games of each other, but during the first two weeks of August the Braves

Jackie Robinson in the Dodger clubhouse on January 18, 1957, shortly after announcing his retirement from baseball. A year later the Dodgers were gone too, leaving Brooklyn fans with two matchless memories. *N.Y. Daily News Photo*

Beneath the scoreboard at Ebbets Field was a sign that read, "Hit sign—win suit. Abe Stark." Thanks to Carl Furillo's skills, Stark awarded very few suits. This photo shows Furillo clutching a fly ball right in front of his number and position on the lineup board. *UPI Photo*

won eleven of twelve games and pulled away from the pack. Behind the hitting of Henry Aaron, Eddie Mathews, and Wes Covington and the pitching of Warren Spahn, Bob Buhl, and Lew Burdette, Milwaukee was a mature and balanced ball club. On September 23, Aaron's forty-third homer, with a man on in the last of the ninth, beat the Cardinals, 4–2, and clinched Milwaukee's first pennant. The Dodgers placed third, their lowest finish since 1948.

As it turned out, the Giants beat the Dodgers to the punch in formally announcing plans to move to California. On August 19, Horace Stoneham stated that his board of directors had voted 9 to 1 in favor of moving the Giants to San Francisco in 1958. The dissenter was M. Donald Grant, who was convinced that National League baseball could operate profitably in New York. He proved it five years later with a diverting group known as the New York Mets. Stoneham said, "We're sorry to disappoint the kids of New York, but we didn't see many of their parents out there at the Polo Grounds in recent years." He predicted that the move would produce annual profits in excess of $200,000, and reported that the Giants had lost money in all but two of the preceding eight seasons.

"It fell to the lot of the Brooklyns to win the opening game of the season at the Polo Grounds yesterday afternoon. The score, 3–2, does not fully tell how close and interesting the game was." This was the lead from the New York *Times*' account of the first game of the 1900 season. The last contests between the Giants and Dodgers were not nearly as close and interesting. They were listless affairs, sparsely attended, and of interest to only the most melancholia-stricken. The Brooks won the last series at Ebbets Field two games to one, and captured two out of three in their concluding set at the Polo Grounds. The Giants won the final New York–Brooklyn game, 3–2, on a two-run homer by Hank Sauer, a veteran slugger purchased during the off-season from the Chicago Cubs. It was the 650th Giant win in the rivalry since 1900, against 606 victories for the Dodgers, but the game was a far cry from the lively clashes of earlier seasons.

The Giants finished fifth for the second season in a row; not even the return of old heroes Bobby Thomson and Whitey Lockman resulted in any improvement. The Polo Grounders dropped their last home game to the Pirates, and at the end of the contest a few thousand spectators jumped onto the field and chased the players all the way to the center-field clubhouse. The mob then tore up the turf, plundered bits and pieces of the bullpens and dugouts, and milled around outside the clubhouse chanting, "We want Willie! We want Willie!" and "We want Stoneham, with a rope around his neck!"

By comparison, Brooklyn rooters were strangely subdued at the conclusion of the Dodgers' final home game. The move to Los Angeles had still not been formally announced at that point, but everyone knew it was coming. The Brooks did manage to end on a winning note, beating Pittsburgh, 3–0. Filing

Before the Giants' last game at the Polo Grounds, Bobby Thomson posed for photographers and pointed to the spot where his "shot heard round the world" landed in the third Giant-Dodger 1951 play-off game. *N.Y. Daily News Photo*

STAY T
STA

This was the scene as the New York Giants clambered up the Polo Grounds clubhouse steps for the last time. Police officers are watching carefully as some fans pursue the players from the field and threaten to dismantle the ball park. *Wide World Photos*

Tom Sturdivant won sixteen games in 1956 and then led Yankee hurlers in 1957 with a 16–6 record and a 2.54 ERA. In his next seven years in the majors he never won more than nine games in a single season. He finished his career in 1964 with the New York Mets. *N.Y. Daily News Photo*

out slowly and quietly, 6,702 of the Faithful took a final, lingering glance at their beloved ball park, while Gladys Goodding played a medley of mournful melodies.

As if concerned that the wheeling and dealing by the Giants and Dodgers might divert attention from them, the Yankees staged some early-season spectaculars that had nothing whatever to do with baseball. In May a group of Bomber regulars staged a table-smashing brawl in the Copacabana that led directly to Billy Martin's expulsion to the Kansas City Athletics. During the first week of June the Yanks invaded Detroit and got into a fight with the Tigers during the second of a three-game series. Then a week later in Chicago a vigorous donnybrook resulted when Yankee pitcher Art Ditmar flattened Larry Doby with a knockdown pitch. Doby rushed the mound and clipped Ditmar with a neat left hook, and then both benches emptied and individual battles broke out, the most spirited involving Chicago's six-foot-five Walt Dropo and five-foot-nine Enos Slaughter, who at forty-one years of age might have been home fishing and enjoying a tranquil retirement.

The White Sox, led by Nelson Fox and Minnie Minoso and the pitching of Billy Pierce, Dick Donovan, and Jim Wilson, stayed close to the Yankees all summer long. On August 27, prior to a three-game series with the Yankees in Chicago, the White Sox were only three and a half games behind the leading Bombers. More than 47,000 eager Chicago fans crammed into Comiskey Park for the opening game, cheered as their team rallied from a 5–0 deficit to a 6–6 tie in the last of the seventh inning, and then groaned as a three-run homer

The Yankees' best reliever in 1957 was Bob Grim, with a 12–8 record and a league-leading total of nineteen saves. He began with the Bombers as a starter in 1954, won twenty games, and was named the American League's Rookie of the Year. *N.Y. Daily News Photo*

by Yogi Berra triggered a six-run outburst and a 12–6 Yankee victory. The Bombers won the next day, 5–4, and then stretched their lead to six and a half games with a third-game 2–1 victory, gained in the top of the eleventh on Enos Slaughter's home run with the bases empty. The New Yorkers clinched the flag on September 23, the same day the Braves were winning the National League pennant.

For the seventh year in a row the World Series opened in New York City. The first game offered a classic pairing of the game's leading southpaw hurlers, Warren Spahn and Whitey Ford. Only an eleven-game winner during the regular season owing to arm troubles, but a matchless competitor in high-stakes contests, Ford won the opener, 3–1, before nearly 70,000 at Yankee Stadium. Whitey was in control throughout, except for some anxious moments in the sixth, when he had to face Hank Aaron, Joe Adcock, and Andy Pafko with two on and nobody out. Ford fanned Aaron on three sharp-breaking curves, retired Adcock on a grounder, and then struck out Pafko to end the threat.

Lew Burdette, whose major-league career began with the Yankees in 1950, countered Ford's effort with a 4–2 complete game win in the second contest. A homer by Johnny Logan helped, as did a running backhanded catch in the second inning by Wes Covington that stole a double from Yankee pitcher Bobby Shantz and prevented two runs from scoring.

It was an important win for the Braves, since the next three games would be played in a madhouse called County Stadium, where clamorous Brave rooters had developed a talent for unsettling the opposition. Just two Mil-

Sal Maglie appeared in six games for the Yankees toward the end of the 1957 season and was credited with two victories. He was over forty years old when this picture was taken, and he appears somewhat ill at ease in a Yankee uniform. *N.Y. Daily News Photo*

Bobby Shantz, on the left, had an 11–5 record in 1957 and led the American League with an ERA of 2.45. Standing next to him is Tony Kubek, the American League Rookie of the Year in 1957. At one time or another during his nine years with the Yankees, Kubek played every position except pitcher and catcher. *N.Y. Daily News Photo*

Milwaukee wins out of three games would return the Series to New York with Bomber backs to the wall.

Ironically, a Milwaukee native was instrumental in frustrating these plans, at least temporarily. American League Rookie of the Year Tony Kubek, with his family and friends looking on, belted a bases-empty home run in the first inning, then added a three-run blast in the fifth. Six Milwaukee pitchers gave up eleven walks, Mickey Mantle hit a two-run homer, and Hank Bauer and Jerry Lumpe had run-scoring hits in the 12–3 laugher. Don Larsen, pitching in his first Series game since his memorable outing against the Dodgers a year earlier, relieved starter Bob Turley in the second inning and went the rest of the way for the win.

Warren Spahn came back in the fourth game, and homers by Aaron and Frank Torre gave him a 4–1 lead going into the top of the ninth. With two on and two out, Spahnie threw Elston Howard a curve ball that hung, Howard rammed it into the seats, and the game was tied. In the top of the tenth a run-scoring triple by Bauer gave the Yankees a 5–4 lead. In real danger of letting the Series get away from them, the Braves sent Nippy Jones up to hit for Spahn in the last of the tenth. Yankee reliever Tommy Byrne threw his first pitch into the dirt at Jones' feet. Plate umpire Augie Donatelli called the pitch a ball, but when Jones showed Donatelli a shoe-polish smudge on the ball, the pinch hitter was awarded first base. Felix Mantilla ran for Jones, was sacrificed to second, and then scored the tying run on Johnny Logan's double. Eddie Mathews followed with a towering shot into the right-field bleachers that won the game, 7–5, and tied the Series at two games apiece.

Burdette's second Series performance was even classier than his first. He won the fifth game, 1–0, allowed seven singles, and permitted just two runners

Elston Howard, the first black man to play in a regular season game for the Yankees, was an able reserve catcher and substitute outfielder. Howard's clutch hits in the 1958 World Series against the Braves helped the Yankees avenge their 1957 Series loss to Milwaukee. *N.Y. Daily News Photo*

to venture as far as second base. Nifty fielding plays by Mathews and Covington bailed him out of two jams, and the only run Burdette needed crossed in the sixth on an infield hit and two bloop singles. The Braves had their two victories in Milwaukee and needed just one in New York for the title.

On the off day reserved for travel, the Dodgers finally announced that they were moving to Los Angeles. The same tired statements were made about dwindling attendance and lack of municipal faith, but the uncomplicated truth was that the California bait was just too juicy for the Dodgers and Giants to pass up. That fact, combined with the circumstances involving outmoded ball parks located in deteriorating neighborhoods with limited parking, hastened the relocations. Parking was especially important, since many fans had moved to the suburbs, well beyond subway access, where it was a lot easier to watch the games on television. O'Malley and Stoneham were very generous with the home-game TV schedule, then neatly justified their transfers on the basis of sagging box-office receipts.

New York's surviving team managed to restore some flagging spirits by evening the World Series the next afternoon at Yankee Stadium, 3–2. Yogi Berra hit a two-run homer in the last of the third that was later equaled by Frank Torre's and Hank Aaron's bases-empty homers. In the last of the seventh Hank Bauer pulled a soft fly ball down the left-field line that caromed off the foul-pole screen for an unmighty but decisive home run. The winning pitcher was Bob Turley, who gave up only four hits.

In the sixth game of the 1957 World Series, with the Milwaukee Braves leading three games to two, Bob Turley pitched a four-hitter and, with home-run help from Yogi Berra and Hank Bauer, beat the Braves, 3–2, and tied the Series. This photo shows Turley pitching to Felix Mantilla in the first inning. *Brown Brothers*

The sixth-game Yankee heroes whoop it up in the clubhouse after tying the 1957 World Series. Hank Bauer, on left, homered in the seventh to break a 2–2 tie, Bob Turley, center, was the winning pitcher, and Yogi Berra hit a two-run homer in the third inning to account for the first Yankee scores. *N.Y. Daily News Photo*

The dynasty is at an end. The Milwaukee Braves have won the 1957 World Series and snapped the New York–Brooklyn dominance after eight years. In this picture Lew Burdette, the winning pitcher, is being embraced by his catcher, Del Crandall, while Eddie Mathews races in to join the happy pair. Heading for their dugout are third-base coach Frank Crosetti and Jerry Coleman, who was forced at third for the final out. *N.Y. Daily News Photo*

Milwaukee manager Fred Haney wanted to use Spahn in the seventh game, but his southpaw ace had the flu, and Haney was forced to go again with Burdette, who was weary from two complete games, the second pitched just two days earlier. Opposing Burdette was Don Larsen, well rested after his impressive showing in the third game. The championship was decided in the top of the third, when Tony Kubek botched a potential inning-ending double play. The error put two runners on with one out, both of whom scored on Eddie Mathews' double. Mathews scored moments later on Aaron's single, and Aaron also scored before the side was retired. In the eighth Del Crandall homered to make the score 5–0. Meanwhile, Burdette was overpowering the Yankees. He walked one batter, gave up just one extra-base hit, and the only threatening situation he faced was in the last of the ninth, with two out and New York runners on first and second. Bill Skowron was the Yankee batter, and he hit a two-hopper to Mathews, who stepped on third for the final out.

The Milwaukee Braves were World Champions, and New York's desolation was complete.

A colorful and unforgettable era had ended. Never again would a city dominate baseball as New York had from 1947 to 1957. No city would boast three major-league teams again: certainly no metropolitan area would ever enjoy such a concentration of gifted and engaging players. Few things last very long, least of all sunny summer afternoons in old neighborhood ball parks. We shall not see the likes of the Yankee Clipper, Yogi, Sal the Barber, Willie, Campy, and Jackie Robinson again.

Appendix

How the teams fared in a number of categories during the 1947–1957 period. The numbers in parentheses indicate how the preceding figure ranked in the league that season. An average figure for stolen bases and complete games has been provided, rather than an eleven-year total.

Table A   Yankees

Year	Mgr.	Fin.	Margin	Won	Lost	Pct.	Batting Avg.	Fielding Avg.	Stolen Bases	Complete Games	ERA	Series Result
1947	Harris	1	+12	97	57	.630	.271(1)	.981(2)	27(8)	73(2)	3.39(1)	Beat Bklyn. 4–3
1948	Harris	3	− 2½	94	60	.610	.278(2)	.978(3)	24(7)	62(4)	3.75(2)	
1949	Stengel	1	+ 1	97	57	.630	.269(2)	.976(4)	58(2)	59(5)	3.69(2)	Beat Bklyn. 4–1
1950	Stengel	1	+ 3	98	56	.636	.282(2)	.979(3)	41(2)	66(3)	4.15(3)	Beat Phils 4–0
1951	Stengel	1	+ 5	98	56	.636	.269(2)	.975(2)	78(2)	66(3)	3.56(3)	Beat Giants 4–2
1952	Stengel	1	+ 2	95	59	.617	.267(1)	.979(1)	52(3)	72(4)	3.32(3)	Beat Bklyn. 4–3
1953	Stengel	1	+ 8½	99	52	.656	.273(1)	.978(3)	34(4)	50(5)	3.20(1)	Beat Bklyn. 4–2
1954	Stengel	2	− 8	103	51	.669	.268(1)	.979(2)	34(5)	51(5)	3.26(3)	
1955	Stengel	1	+ 3	96	58	.623	.260(5)	.978(3)	55(2)	52(3)	3.23(1)	Lost to Bklyn. 4–3
1956	Stengel	1	+ 9	97	57	.630	.270(3)	.977(3)	51(2)	50(4)	3.63(2)	Beat Bklyn. 4–3
1957	Stengel	1	+ 8	98	56	.636	.268(1)	.979(3)	49(3)	41(6)	3.00(1)	Lost to Milw. 4–3
Totals				1072	619	.634	.270	.978	46	58	3.47	Won 7 Series, Lost 2
												Won 30 Games, Lost 22

Table B   Dodgers

Year	Mgr.	Fin.	Margin	Won	Lost	Pct.	Batting Avg.	Fielding Avg.	Stolen Bases	Complete Games	ERA	Series Result
1947	Sukeforth (1)											
	Shotton (153)	1	+ 5	94	60	.610	.272(2)	.978(2)	88(1)	47(6)	3.82(3)	Lost to Yanks 4–3
1948	Durocher (73)											
	Shotton (81)	3	− 7½	84	70	.545	.261(4)	.973(4)	114(1)	52(6)	3.75(2)	
1949	Shotton	1	+ 1	97	57	.623	.274(2)	.979(1)	117(1)	62(3)	3.80(2)	Lost to Yanks 4–1
1950	Shotton	2	− 2	89	65	.578	.272(1)	.978(1)	77(1)	62(4)	4.28(5)	
1951	Dressen	2	− 1	97	60	.618	.275(1)	.979(2)	89(1)	64(2)	3.88(5)	
1952	Dressen	1	+ 4½	96	57	.627	.256(3)	.982(1)	90(1)	45(6)	3.53(2)	Lost to Yanks 4–3
1953	Dressen	1	+13	105	49	.682	.285(1)	.979(1)	90(1)	51(3)	4.10(3)	Lost to Yanks 4–2
1954	Alston	2	− 5	92	62	.597	.270(2)	.978(2)	46(4)	39(5)	4.31(4)	
1955	Alston	1	+13½	98	55	.641	.271(1)	.977(2)	79(1)	46(6)	3.68(1)	Beat Yanks 4–3
1956	Alston	1	+ 1	93	61	.604	.258(4)	.981(1)	65(2)	46(4)	3.57(2)	Lost to Yanks 4–3
1957	Alston	3	−11	84	70	.545	.253(5)	.978(3)	60(2)	44(5)	3.35(1)	
Totals				1029	666	.607	.268	.978	83	51	3.82	Won 1 Series, Lost 5
												Won 16 games, lost 23

Table C Giants

Year	Mgr.		Fin.	Margin	Won	Lost	Pct.	Batting Avg.	Fielding Avg.	Stolen Bases	Complete Games	ERA	Series Result
1947	Ott		4	13	81	73	.526	.271(3)	.974(4)	29(6)	58(4)	4.44(7)	
1948	Ott (65)												
	Durocher	(89)	5	−13½	78	76	.506	.256(7)	.973(4)	51(3)	54(5)	3.93(4)	
1949	Durocher		5	−24	73	81	.474	.261(3)	.972(7)	43(4)	68(1)	3.82(3)	
1950	Durocher		3	− 5	86	68	.558	.258(6)	.977(3)	42(5)	70(2)	3.71(2)	
1951	Durocher		1	+ 1	98	59	.624	.260(4)	.972(7)	55(5)	64(2)	3.48(1)	Lost to Yanks 4–2
1952	Durocher		2	− 4½	92	62	.597	.256(5)	.973(5)	30(8)	49(5)	3.59(4)	
1953	Durocher		5	−35	70	84	.455	.271(3)	.974(5)	31(6)	46(6)	4.25(5)	
1954	Durocher		1	+ 5	97	57	.630	.264(5)	.974(5)	30(5)	45(3)	3.09(2)	Beat Cleve. 4–0
1955	Durocher		3	−18½	80	74	.519	.260(4)	.976(3)	38(6)	52(3)	3.77(2)	
1956	Rigney		6	−26	67	87	.435	.244(7)	.975(5)	67(1)	31(7)	3.78(4)	
1957	Rigney		6	−26	69	85	.448	.252(6)	.973(6)	64(1)	35(7)	4.01(6)	
Totals					891	806	.525	.259	.974	44	52	3.81	Won 1 Series, Lost 1 Won 6 games, Lost 4

Table D Champions

The extent to which New York players dominated the important hitting and pitching categories, as well as the Rookie of the Year and Most Valuable Player awards.

Year	Batting	Home Runs	RBIs.	20-game Winners	Saves	ERA	Rookie of the Year	MVP	League
1947		Mize 51*	Mize 138	Branca 21–12	Casey 18		Robinson		NL
				Jansen 21–5					
1948					Page 17*	Chandler 2.46		DiMaggio	AL
		Mize 40*							NL
		DiMaggio 39	DiMaggio 155						AL
1949	Robinson .342					Koslo 2.50	Newcombe	Robinson	NL
				Raschi 21–10	Page 27				AL
1950						Hearn 2.48			NL
				Raschi 21–8				Rizzuto	AL
1951			Irvin 121	Roe 22–3			Mays	Campanella	NL
				Newcombe 20–9					
				Maglie 23–6					
				Jansen 23–11					
				Lopat 21–9			McDougald	Berra	AL
				Raschi 21–10					
1952						Wilhelm 2.43	Black		NL
				Reynolds 20–8		Reynolds 2.06			AL
1953	Furillo .344		Campanella 142	Erskine 20–6			Gilliam	Campanella	NL
						Lopat 2.42			AL
1954	Mays .345			Antonelli 21–7		Wilhelm 2.10		Mays	NL
				Grim 20–6	Sain 22		Grim	Berra	AL
1955		Mays 51	Snider 136	Newcombe 20–5				Campanella	NL
		Mantle 37						Berra	AL
1956		Snider 43		Newcombe 27–7	Labine 19			Newcombe	NL
				Antonelli 20–13					
	Mantle .353	Mantle 52	Mantle 130			Ford 2.47		Mantle	AL
1957					Labine 17	Podres 2.66			NL
					Grim 19	Shantz 2.45	Kubek	Mantle	AL

*Tie

A selection of the twelve best players from each team during the years 1947–1957. The first line shows the totals for each player during the time span, the second his best year within the period, the third gives totals for World Series play from 1947 through 1957, and the fourth line is the player's lifetime statistics.

Table E   Yankees

Name		Years	Games	Avg.	Hrs.	RBIs	Games by position
Hank Bauer	10	(48–57)	1145	.282	137	565	1113–OF–1–C
Best year		1956	147	.241	26	84	146–OF
Series		8	46	.229	3	16	45–OF
Lifetime	14	(48–61)	1544	.277	164	703	1449–OF 1–C
Yogi Berra	11	(47–57)	1467	.290	260	1081	1343–C 81–OF 1–3B
Best year		1954	151	.307	22	125	149–C 1–3B
Series		9	54	.281	10	26	52–C 2–OF
Lifetime	19	(46–65)	2120	.285	358	1430	1696–C 260–OF 1–3B 2–1B
Joe DiMaggio	5	(47–51)	625	.325	117	512	617–OF 1–1B
Best Year		1948	153	.320	39	155	152–OF
Series		4	22	.225	5	14	22–OF
Lifetime	13	(36–51)	1736	.325	361	1537	1721–OF 1–1B
Tommy Henrich	4	(47–50)	476	.293	71	317	295–OF 138–1B
Best year		1948	146	.308	25	100	102–OF 46–1B
Series		2	12	.300	2	26	7–OF 5–1B
Lifetime	11	(37–50)	1284	.282	183	795	1017–OF 189–1B
Mickey Mantle	7	(51–57)	952	.316	207	669	920–OF 7–SS 1–2B 1–3B
Best year		1956	150	.353	52	130	144–OF
Series		6	31	.261	9	17	29–OF
Lifetime	18	(51–68)	2401	.298	536	1509	2019–OF 262–1B 7–SS 1–2B 1–3B
Gil McDougald	7	(51–57)	952	.285	86	443	399–3B 389–2B 213–SS
Best year		1951	131	.306	14	63	82–3B 55–2B
Series		6	40	.215	5	18	25–3B 14–SS 4–2B
Lifetime	10	(51–60)	1336	.276	112	576	599–2B 508–3B 284–SS
Phil Rizzuto	10	(47–56)	1258	.269	29	410	1250–SS 2–2B
Best year		1950	155	.324	7	66	155–SS
Series		7	42	.243	1	7	42–SS
Lifetime	13	(41–56)	1661	.273	38	562	1647–SS 2–2B
Gene Woodling	6	(49–54)	698	.285	51	336	658–OF
Best year		1952	122	.309	12	63	118–OF
Series		5	26	.318	3	6	24–OF
Lifetime	17	(43–62)	1796	.284	147	830	1569–OF

			IP	Won	Lost	Hits	Walks	ERA
Whitey Ford	6	(50–57)	180	1138	91	33	933	513	2.72
Best year		1956	31	225.2	19	6	187	84	2.47
Series		5	9	62	5	3	54	18	3.31
Lifetime	16	(50–67)	498	3170.1	236	106	2766	1086	2.75

			IP	Won	Lost	Hits	Walks	ERA
Ed Lopat	8	(48–55)	217	1411	113	59	1406	389	3.11
Best year		1951	31	234.2	21	9	209	71	2.91
Series		5	7	52	4	1	51	12	2.60
Lifetime	12	(44–55)	340	2439.1	166	112	2464	650	3.21
Vic Raschi	7	(47–53)	216	1521	118	50	1333	615	3.49
Best year		1951	35	258.1	21	10	233	103	3.27
Series		6	11	60.1	5	3	52	25	2.24
Lifetime	10	(46–55)	269	1819	132	66	1666	727	3.72
Allie Reynolds	8	(47–54)	295	1700	131	60	1500	819	3.32
Best year		1952	35	244.1	20	8	194	97	2.06
Series		6	15	77.1	7	2	61	32	2.79
Lifetime	13	(42–54)	434	2492.1	182	107	2193	1261	3.30

Table F   Dodgers

Name		Years	Games	Avg.	Hrs.	RBIs	Games by position
Billy Cox	7	(48–54)	742	.259	46	245	663–3B 40–SS 35–2B
Best year		1951	142	.279	9	51	139–3B 1–SS
Series		3	15	.302	1	6	14–3B
Lifetime	11	(41–55)	1058	.262	66	351	700–3B 299–SS 53–2B
Roy Campanella	10	(48–57)	1215	.276	242	856	1183 C
Best year		1953	144	.312	41	142	140 C
Series		5	32	.237	4	12	32 C
Lifetime (see first line)							
Carl Furillo	11	(47–57)	1509	.302	171	926	1481 OF
Best year		1953	132	.344	21	92	131 OF
Series		6	36	.267	2	11	35 OF
Lifetime	15	(46–60)	1806	.299	192	1058	1739 OF
Jim Gilliam	5	(53–57)	746	.272	34	235	641–2B 109–OF
Best year		1956	153	.300	6	43	102–2B 56–OF
Series		3	20	.227	2	9	17–2B 3–OF
Lifetime	14	(53–66)	1956	.265	65	558	1046–2B 761–3B 224–OF 2–1B
Gil Hodges	11	(47–57)	1530	.279	308	1049	1424–1B 70–OF 63–C 2–3B 1–2B
Best year		1954	154	.304	42	130	154–1B
Series		6	33	.241	4	19	32–1B
Lifetime	18	(43–63)	2071	.273	370	1274	1908–1B 79–OF 64–C 32–3B 1–2B
Peewee Reese	11	(47–57)	1568	.274	107	681	1455–SS 94–3B
Best year		1949	155	.279	16	73	155–SS
Series		6	39	.282	2	14	39–SS
Lifetime	16	(40–58)	2166	.269	126	885	2016–SS 115–3B
Jackie Robinson	10	(47–56)	1382	.311	137	734	751–2B 256–3B 197–1B 152–OF 1–SS
Best year		1949	156	.342	16	124	156–2B
Series		6	38	.234	2	12	13–3B 12–2B 7–1B 6–OF
Lifetime (see first line)							

Name		Years	Games	Avg.	Hrs.	RBIs	Games by position
Duke Snider	11	(47–57)	1425	.303	316	1003	1390–OF
Best year		1955	148	.309	42	136	146–OF
Series		5	32	.293	10	24	32–OF
Lifetime	18	(47–64)	2143	.295	407	1333	1918–OF

Name		Years	Games	IP	Won	Lost	Hits	Walks	ERA
Carl Erskine	10	(48–57)	294	1597	118	71	1489	598	3.90
Best year		1953	39	246.2	20	6	189	57	3.54
Series		5	11	41.2	2	2	36	24	5.83
Lifetime	12	(48–59)	335	1718.2	122	78	1637	646	4.00
Clem Labine	8	(50–57)	304	727	59	35	659	275	3.60
Best year		1956	62	115.2	10	6	111	39	3.35
Series		4	9	26	2	2	24	6	3.25
Lifetime	13	(50–62)	513	1079.2	77	56	1043	396	3.63
Don Newcombe	7	(49–57)	247	1628	123	60	1514	405	3.49
Best year		1956	38	268	27	7	219	46	3.06
Series		3	5	22	0	4	29	8	8.59
Lifetime	10	(49–60)	344	2154.2	149	90	2102	490	3.56
Preacher Roe	7	(48–54)	201	1277	93	37	1252	309	3.46
Best year		1951	34	257.2	22	3	247	64	3.04
Series		3	5	28.1	2	1	20	10	2.54
Lifetime	12	(38–54)	333	1914.2	127	84	1907	504	3.43

Table G Giants

Name		Years	Games	Avg.	Hrs.	RBIs	Games by Position
Alvin Dark	7	(50–56)	933	.292	98	429	887–SS 26–2B 17–OF 1–P
Best year		1953	155	.300	23	88	110–SS 26–2B 17–OF 8–3B 1–P
Series		3	16	.323	1	4	16–SS
Lifetime	14	(46–60)	1828	.289	126	757	1404–SS 320–3B 43–OF 29–2B 15–1B 1–P
Monte Irvin	7	(49–55)	653	.296	84	393	489–OF 104–1B 7–3B
Best year		1951	151	.312	24	121	112–OF 39–1B
Series		2	10	.394	0	4	10–OF
Lifetime	8	(49–56)	764	.293	99	443	585–OF 104–1B 7–3B
Whitey Lockman	11	(47–57)	1361	.277	108	518	645–OF 708–1B
Best year		1949	151	.301	11	65	151–OF
Series		2	10	.302	1	4	10–1B
Lifetime	15	(45–60)	1666	.279	114	563	771–1B 752–OF 26–2B 1–3B
Willie Mays	6	(51–57)	762	.311	187	509	760–OF
Best year		1955	152	.319	51	127	152–OF
Series		2	10	.211	0	4	10–OF
Lifetime	22	(51–73)	2990	.302	660	1903	2813–OF 146–1B 2–SS 1–3B

Name		Years	Games	Avg.	Hrs.	RBIs	Games by Position
Johnny Mize	3	(47–49)	412	.287	109	325	412–1B
Best year		1947	154	.302	51	138	154–1B
Series*	5		18	.286	3	9	10–1B * with Yankees
Lifetime	15	(36–53)	1884	.312	359	1337	1667–1B 8–OF
Don Mueller	10	(48–57)	1171	.298	65	504	1041–OF
Best year		1954	153	.342	4	71	153–OF
Series	1		4	.389	0	1	4–OF
Lifetime	12	(48–59)	1245	.296	65	520	1084–OF
Hank Thompson	8	(49–56)	906	.267	129	477	655–3B 102–OF 83–2B 2–SS
Best year		1953	114	.302	24	74	101–3B 9–OF 1–2B
Series	2		9	.240	0	2	5–OF 4–3B
Lifetime	9	(48–56)	933	.267	129	482	655–3B 102–OF 102–2B 2–SS
Bobby Thomson	8	(47–53, 57)	1117	.277	187	695	931–OF 161–3B 9–2B
Best year		1949	156	.309	27	109	156–OF
Series	1		6	.238	0	2	6–3B
Lifetime	15	(46–60)	1779	.270	264	1026	1506–OF 184–3B 9–2B 1–1B

Name		Years	Games	IP	Won	Lost	Hits	Walks	ERA
Johnny Antonelli	4	(54–57)	158	964	67	54	868	318	3.07
Best year		1954	39	258.2	21	7	209	94	2.30
Series	1		2	10.2	1	0	8	7	0.84
Lifetime	12	(48–61)	377	1992.1	126	110	1870	687	3.34
Larry Jansen	8	(47–54)	283	1731	120	86	1712	401	3.86
Best year		1951	39	278.1	23	11	254	56	3.04
Series	1		3	10	0	2	8	4	6.30
Lifetime	9	(47–54, 56)	291	1765.1	122	89	1751	410	3.58
Sal Maglie	6	(50–55)	208	1214	90	38	1144	412	3.86
Best year		1951	42	298	23	6	254	86	2.93
Series	3 (1 w. Bk.)		4	29	1	2	29	10	3.41
Lifetime	10	(45, 50–58)	303	1723	119	62	1591	562	3.15
Hoyt Wilhelm	5	(52–56)	319	608	42	25	532	269	3.07
Best year		1952	71	159.1	15	3	127	57	2.43
Series	1		2	2.1	0	0	1	0	0.00
Lifetime	21	(52–72)	1070	2253	143	122	1757	778	2.52

Table H   Attendance

The annual attendance figures for each team

	Yankees	Dodgers	Giants
1947	2,200,369	1,807,596	1,599,784
1948	2,373,901	1,398,967	1,459,269
1949	2,283,676	1,633,747	1,218,446
1950	2,081,375	1,185,099	1,009,951
1951	1,950,107	1,282,628	1,059,539
1952	1,629,665	1,088,704	984,940
1953	1,538,007	1,163,419	811,519
1954	1,475,171	1,020,531	1,155,067
1955	1,490,138	1,033,589	824,112
1956	1,491,594	1,213,562	629,267
1957	1,497,134	1,026,158	653,903

Table I   Giants-Dodgers Season Series Results

The Giant-Dodger rivalry. How the teams did against each other from 1947 through 1957. Three extra games were needed to decide the 1951 pennant.

	Bklyn	*NY*		*Bklyn*	*NY*
1947	14	8	1953	15	7
1948	11	11	1954	9	13
1949	14	8	1955	13	9
1950	12	10	1956	14	8
1951	14	11	1957	12	10
1952	8	14	TOTAL	136	109

Table J   Hall of Fame

The roster of players and other notables who performed during the period. Barring an extraordinary circumstance, Willie Mays' admission will be a formality.

Yogi Berra	Willie Mays (in 1979)
Roy Campanella	Mel Ott
Joe DiMaggio	Branch Rickey
Whitey Ford	Jackie Robinson
Monte Irvin	Casey Stengel
Sandy Koufax	George Weiss
Mickey Mantle	